TABLE OF CONTENTS

Trout-Perch Family

WHAT'S NEW IN THE SECOND EDITION

First released in 2007, *Fish of Michigan* has made fish identification easy for experienced anglers and rookies alike. Now with over 79 species, this revised and expanded edition offers even more for anglers and those who spend time around the water. Here's what is new in the second edition.

More Species: Six additional species have been added to this book; several are aquatic invasive species, so it's especially important to be on the lookout for them. The new species are Silver and Bighead Carp, Round Goby, Ruffe, Bigmouth Buffalo, and White Bass Hybrid.

Fishing Tips: Popular game species now feature fishing tips to help you catch more fish.

Revised and Updated: Whether it's new state fish records, the latest details about the spread of invasive species, or fish range changes, the new *Fish of Michigan* has been brought up to date with all the latest information available.

The Same Stuff You Know and Love: As before, the new book features world-class illustrations and lots of fascinating facts about each species, as well as all the new information.

HOW TO USE THIS BOOK

The fish are organized by families (such as Catfish, Minnow, Perch, Pike, Salmon and Sunfish), which are listed in alphabetical order. Within these families, individual species are also arranged alphabetically, in groups where necessary. For example, members of the Sunfish family are divided into Black Bass, Crappie, and True Sunfish groups. For a detailed list of fish families and individual species, turn to the Table of Contents (pg. 3); the Index (pg. 166) provides a handy reference guide to fish by common name (such as Lake Trout) and other common terms used in the book.

Fish Identification

Determining a fish's body shape is the first step in identifying it. Each fish family usually exhibits one, or sometimes two, basic outlines. Catfish have long, stout bodies with flattened heads, barbels or "whiskers" around the mouth, a relatively tall but narrow dorsal fin, and an adipose fin. There are two forms of sunfish: the flat, round, plate-like outline we see in Bluegills; and the torpedo or "fusiform" shape of bass.

In this field guide you can quickly identify your catch by first matching its general body shape to one of the fish family silhouettes listed in the Table of Contents (pg. 3). From there, turn to that family's section and use the illustrations and text descriptions to identify your fish. A sample (pg. 22) is provided to explain how the information is presented in each two-page spread.

For some species, the illustration will be enough to identify your catch, but it is important to note that your fish may not look exactly like the picture. Fish frequently change colors. Males that are brightly colored during the spawning season may be dull silver at other times. Similarly, fish caught in muddy streams show much less pattern than those taken from clear lakes—and all fish lose some of their markings and color when they are out of the water for a little while. Most fish are similar in appearance to one or more other species—often, but not always, within the same family. For example, the Black Crappie is remarkably similar to its cousin, the White Crappie. To accurately identify such look-alikes, check the inset illustrations and accompanying notes below the main illustration, under the "Similar Species" heading.

Throughout *Fish of Michigan*, we use basic biological and fisheries management terms that refer to physical characteristics or conditions of fish and their environment, such as "dorsal fin" or "turbid water." For your convenience, these terms are defined in the Glossary (pg. 160) along with other handy fish-related terms and their definitions. Understanding such terminology will help you make sense of state and federal research reports, population surveys, lake assessments, management plans, and other fish-related documents.

FISH ANATOMY

To identify fish, you will need to know a few basic terms that apply to fins and their locations.

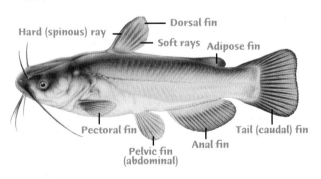

Hard (spinous) ray — Dorsal fin

Soft rays — Adipose fin

Pectoral fin

Pelvic fin (abdominal)

Anal fin

Tail (caudal) fin

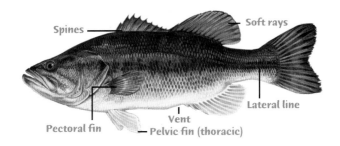

Spines — Soft rays
Lateral line
Pectoral fin — Vent
Pelvic fin (thoracic)

Fins are made up of bony structures that support a membrane. There are three kinds of bony structures in fins. **Soft rays** are flexible fin supports that are sometimes branched. **Spines** are stiff, often sharp, supports that are not jointed. **Hard rays** are stiff, pointed, barbed structures that can be raised or lowered. Catfish are famous for their hard rays, which are mistakenly called spines. Sunfish have soft rays associated with spines to form a dorsal fin.

Fins are named by their position on the fish. The **dorsal fin** is on the top along the midline. A few fish have another fin on their back called an **adipose fin**. This is a small, fleshy protuberance located between the dorsal fin and the tail and is distinctive of trout and catfish.

On each side of the fish near the gills are the **pectoral fins**. The **anal fin** is located along the midline on the fish's bottom or ventral side. There is also a paired set of fins on the bottom of the fish called the **pelvic fins**. Pelvic fins can be in the **thoracic position** just below the pectoral fins or farther back on the stomach in the **abdominal position**. The tail is known as the **caudal fin**.

Eyes—In general, fish have good eyesight. They can see color, but the light level they require to see well varies by species. For example, Walleyes see well in low light, whereas Bluegills have excellent daytime vision but see poorly at night, making them vulnerable to predation. Catfish have poor vision both night and day.

Nostrils—A pair of nostrils, or nares, is used to detect odors in the water. Eels and catfish have particularly well-developed senses of smell.

Mouth—The shape of the mouth is a clue to what the fish eats. The larger the food it consumes, the larger the mouth.

Teeth—Not all fish have teeth, but those that do have teeth use them to feed. Walleyes, northern pike, and muskies have sharp canine teeth for grabbing and holding prey. Minnows have teeth—located in the throat and used for grinding. Catfish have cardiform teeth, which feel like a rough patch in the front of the mouth. Bass have tiny patches of vomerine teeth in the roof of the mouth.

Swim Bladder—Almost all fish have a swim bladder, a balloon-like organ that helps the fish regulate its buoyancy.

Lateral Line—This sensory organ helps the fish detect movement in the water (to help avoid predators or capture prey) as well as water currents and pressure changes. It consists of fluid-filled sacs with hair-like sensors, which are open to the water through a row of pores in the skin along each side. These pores create a visible line down the middle of the fish's side.

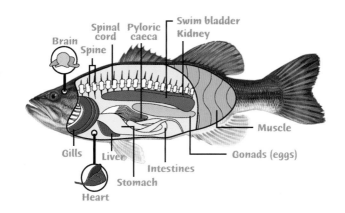

FISH NAMES

A Walleye is a Walleye in Michigan, where it's revered as a game fish. But in the northern parts of its range, Canadians call it a jack or jackfish. And in the eastern United States it is often grouped with other pike-shaped fish and called a pickerel or walleyed pike.

Because common names may vary regionally, and even change for different sizes of the same species, scientific names are used that are exactly the same around the world. Each species has only one correct scientific name that can be recognized anywhere, in any language. The Walleye is *Sander vitreus* from Marquette to Moscow.

Scientific names are made up of Greek or Latin words that often describe the species. There are two parts to a scientific name, the generic or "genus," which is capitalized (*Sander*), and the specific name, which is not capitalized (*vitreus*). Scientific names are displayed in italic text or underlined.

A species' genus represents a group of closely related fish. The Walleye and the Sauger are in the same genus, so they share the generic name *Sander*. But each have different specific names, *vitreus* for Walleye, *canadensis* for the Sauger. Thus the full scientific name for Walleye is *Sander vitreus* and *Sander canadenses* for the Sauger.

ABOUT MICHIGAN FISH

Michigan possesses four times more water than any other of the 48 contiguous states. There are 3,000 miles of Great Lakes coastline, 11,000 inland lakes, and 36,000 miles of rivers and streams. The large diversity of waters provides an almost unlimited number of habitats for freshwater fish, and a profusion of opportunities to watch, study, and pursue them.

There are approximately 154 species of fish in Michigan. Of these, about 30 are the primary targets for anglers. Another 40-plus species are of particular interest to those who spend time near the water, either because they are important bait-fish, aquatic invaders, or just interesting fish you are likely to run into. Together, these species provide an introduction to Michigan's fish that you will find in this book.

FREQUENTLY ASKED QUESTIONS

What is a fish?

Fish are aquatic, typically cold-blooded animals that have backbones, gills, and fins.

Are all fish cold-blooded?

All freshwater fish are cold-blooded. Recently, it has been discovered that a few saltwater fish, including some members of the Tuna family, are warm-blooded. Whales and Bottlenose Dolphins are also warm-blooded, but they are mammals, not fish.

Do all fish have scales?

No. Most fish have scales that look like those on the Common Goldfish. A few, such as Longnose Gar, have scales that resemble armor plates. Catfish have no scales at all.

How do fish breathe?

A fish takes in water through its mouth and forces it through its gills, where a system of fine membranes absorbs oxygen from the water and releases carbon dioxide. Gills cannot pump air efficiently over these membranes, which quickly dry out and stick together. Fish should never be out of the water longer than you can hold your breath.

Can fish breathe air?

Some species can; gar have a modified swim bladder that acts like a lung. Fish that can't breathe air may die when dissolved oxygen in the water falls below critical levels.

How do fish swim?

Fish swim by contracting bands of muscles on alternate sides of their body so the tail is whipped rapidly from side to side. Pectoral and pelvic fins are used mainly for stability when a fish hovers but are sometimes used during rapid bursts of forward motion.

Do all fish look like fish?

Most do and are easily recognizable as fish. The eels and lampreys are fish, but they look like snakes. Sculpins look like little goblins with bat wings.

Where can you find fish?

Some fish species can be found in almost any body of water, but not all fish are found everywhere. Each species has adapted to exploit a particular habitat. A species may move around within its home water, sometimes migrating hundreds of miles between lakes, rivers, and tributary streams. Some movements, such as spawning migrations, are seasonal and very predictable.

Fish may also move horizontally from one area to another, or vertically in the water column, in response to changes in environmental conditions and food availability. In addition, many fish have daily travel patterns. By studying a species' habitat, food, and spawning information in this book—and understanding how it interacts with other Michigan fish—it is possible to make an educated prediction of where to find it in any lake, stream, or river.

FISH DISEASES

Fish are susceptible to various parasites, infections, and diseases. Some diseases have little effect on fish populations, while others may have a devastating impact. While fish diseases can't be transmitted to humans, they may render the fish inedible. To prevent the spread of such diseases, don't transfer any fish from one body of water to another. Information on Michigan fish diseases can be found at the DNR website www.michigan.gov/dnr/

INVASIVE SPECIES

While some introduced species have great recreational value (Rainbow Trout, for example), many exotic species have caused problems. Helping limit the spread of these nuisance species is everyone's responsibility. Never move fish, water, or vegetation from one lake or stream to another, and always follow state recommendations on protecting our state's waters. Details about aquatic invasive species are available at the Michigan DNR website: www.michigan.gov/dnr/invasive

FUN WITH FISH

There are many ways to enjoy Michigan's fish, from reading about them in this book to watching them in the wild. Hands-on activities are also popular. Many resident and nonresident anglers enjoy pursuing Michigan's game fish. The sport offers a great chance to enjoy the outdoors with friends and family and, in many cases, bring home a healthy meal of fresh fish.

Proceeds from license sales, along with special taxes anglers pay on fishing supplies and motorboat fuel, fund the majority of fish management efforts, including fish surveys, the development of special regulations, and stocking programs. The sport also has a huge impact on Michigan's economy, supporting thousands of jobs in fishing, tourism, and related industries.

CATCH-AND-RELEASE FISHING

Selective harvest (keeping some fish to eat and releasing the rest) and total catch-and-release fishing allow anglers to enjoy the sport without harming the resource. Catch-and-release is especially important with certain species and sizes of fish, and in lakes or rivers where biologists are trying to improve the fishery by protecting adult fish of breeding age. Many lakes now have mandatory slot limits requiring anglers to release fish of a certain length. Before you head out, check the DNR's website for slot limits on the lakes you'll be fishing: www.michigan.gov/dnr/

Catch-and-release is only truly successful if the fish survives the experience. Here are some helpful tips to reduce the chances of post-release mortality:

- Play and land fish quickly.
- Wet your hands before touching a fish to avoid removing its protective slime coating.
- Handle the fish gently and keep it in the water as much as possible.
- Do not hold the fish by the eyes or gills. Hold it by the lower lip or under the gill plate—and support its belly.
- If a fish is deeply hooked, cut the line so at least an inch hangs outside the mouth. This helps the hook lie flat when the fish takes in food.
- Circle hooks may help reduce the number of deeply hooked fish.
- Avoid fishing in deep water unless you plan to keep your catch.

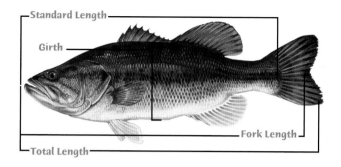

FISH MEASUREMENT

The are three ways to measure fish: standard length (from the tip of the snout to just before the tail), fork length (from the tip of the snout to the middle of the tail fork), and total length. The first two are more accurate because tails are often damaged. In Michigan, total length is used in slot limits; it's also what anglers commonly measure. To measure a fish's total length, pinch the tail together to make the fish as long as possible. The following formulas estimate the weight of popular fish. The total length is in inches; weight is in pounds.

Formulas

Bass weight = (length x length x girth) / 1,200
Pike weight = (length x length x length) / 3,500
Sunfish weight = (length x length x length) / 1,200
Trout weight = (length x girth x girth) / 800
Walleye weight = (length x length x length) / 2,700

Let's say that you catch a 16-inch Walleye. Using the formula for Walleyes above: (16 x 16 x 16) divided by 2,700 = 1.5 pounds. Your Walleye would weigh approximately 1.5 pounds.

MICHIGAN STATE RECORD FISH

SPECIES	WEIGHT (LBS.)	LENGTH (IN.)	WHERE CAUGHT	YEAR
Bass, Largemouth	11.94 (tie)	27.00	Alcona Dam	1959
			Big Pine Island L.	1934
Bass, Rock	3.62	20.00	Holloway Reservoir	1965
Bass, Smallmouth	9.98	23.10	Indian River	2016
Bass, White	6.44	21.90	Saginaw Bay	1989
Bowfin	14.00	35.00	Crooked Lake	1981
Buffalo, Bigmouth	33.00	36.25	Lake Erie	2020
Buffalo, Black	46.54	38.50	Grand River	2018
Bullhead, Black	3.44	17.00	Magician Lake	1999
Bullhead, Brown	3.77	17.50	Alcona Dam Pond	2014
Bullhead, Yellow	3.60	16.80	Lake Sixteen	2003
Burbot	18.25	40.00	St. Mary's River	1980
Carp, Common	61.50	47.50	Wolf Lake	1974
Catfish, Channel	40.00	41.50	Houghton Lake	1964
Catfish, Flathead	52.00	46.00	Barron Lake	2014
Crappie, Black	4.12	N/A	Lincoln Lake	1947
Crappie, White	3.39	19.50	Stony Creek Lake	2000
Drum, Freshwater	28.61	34.00	Muskegon Lake	2015
Eel, American	7.44	43.00	Lake St. Clair	1990
Gar, Longnose	18.00	53.00	Williamsville Lake	1995
Hybrid Bass, White	10.75	27.50	Kalamazoo River	1996
Mooneye	1.69	14.30	Lake St. Clair	1995
Muskellunge (Northern)	49.75	51.00	Thornapple Lake	2000
Muskellunge (Great Lakes)	58.00	59.00	Lake Bellaire	2012
Muskellunge, Tiger	51.19	54.00	Lac Vieux Desert	1919
Perch, White	2.00	13.57	Bear Lake	2015
Perch, Yellow	3.75	21.00	Lake Independence	1947
Pike, Northern	39.00	51.50	Dodge Lake	1961
Quillback	9.15	24.75	Muskegon River	2020
Redhorse, River	12.89	29.20	Muskegon River	1991
Salmon, Atlantic	32.62	41.00	Lake Michigan	1981
Salmon, Chinook	46.06	43.50	Grand River	1978
Salmon, Coho	30.56	40.00	Platte River	1976
Salmon, Kokanee	1.94	18.00	Clinton River	1978
Salmon, Pink	8.56	28.00	Carp River	1987
Sauger	6.56	25.50	Torch Lake	1976
Shad, Gizzard	4.12	21.00	Lake St. Clair	1996

SPECIES	WEIGHT (LBS.)	LENGTH (IN.)	WHERE CAUGHT	YEAR
Splake	17.50	34.50	Lake Michigan	2004
Sturgeon, Lake	193.00	87.00	Mullett Lake	1974
Sucker, Northern Hog	2.54	19.00	St. Joseph River	1994
Sucker, Longnose	6.88	22.50	St. Joseph River	1986
Sucker, White	7.19	28.00	Au Sable River	1982
Sunfish, Bluegill	2.75	13.75	Vaughn Lake	1983
Sunfish, Green	1.53	10.00	Kirkwood Lake	1990
Sunfish, Pumpkinseed	2.15	12.60	Lake Nepessing	2009
Sunfish, Redear	2.36	12.60	Lyon Lake	2010
Trout, Brook	9.50	28.10	Clear Lake	1996
Trout, Brown	41.45	43.70	Manistee River	2009
Trout, Lake	61.50	49.00	Lake Superior	1997
Trout, Rainbow	26.50	39.50	Lake Michigan	1975
Walleye	17.19	35.00	Pine River	1951
Warmouth	1.38	11.00	Great Bear Lake	2001
Whitefish, Lake	14.28	31.75	Lake Superior	1993
Whitefish, Round	4.06	21.50	Lake Michigan	1992

FISH CONSUMPTION ADVISORIES

Most fish are safe to eat, but pollutants are a valid concern. Michigan routinely monitors contaminant levels and issues advisories and recommendations about eating sport fish caught in the wild. For up-to-date fish consumption guidelines where you're fishing in Michigan, visit: Michigan Department of Health: michigan.gov/eatsafefish

These pages explain how the information is presented for each fish.

SAMPLE FISH ILLUSTRATION

Description: brief summary of physical characteristics, such as coloration, markings, body shape, fin size and placement

Similar Species: lists other fish that look similar and the pages on which they can be found; also includes detailed inset drawings (below) highlighting physical traits such as markings, mouth size or shape and fin characteristics to help you distinguish this fish from similar species

Brook Trout	**Brown Trout**	**Rainbow Trout**	**Lake Trout**
worm-like marks, red spots	large dark spots, small red dots	pink stripe on silver body	sides lack red spots

Brook Trout	**Lake Trout**	**Splake**
tail square to slightly forked	tail deeply forked	tail moderately forked

22

COMMON NAME
Scientific Name

Other Names: common terms or nicknames you may hear to describe this species

Habitat: environment where the fish is found (such as streams, rivers, small or large lakes, fast-flowing or still water, in or around vegetation, near shore, in clear water)

Range: geographic distribution, starting with the fish's overall range, followed by state-specific information

Food: what the fish eats most of the time (such as crustaceans, insects, fish, plankton)

Reproduction: timing of and behavior during the spawning period (dates and water temperatures, migration information, preferred spawning habitat, type of nest if applicable, colonial or solitary nester, parental care for eggs or fry)

Record and Average Size: Michigan state record if applicable, see page 20 for a listing of Michigan state records; the average size of fish caught in Michigan

Fishing ◐ Tip: tips to help you catch more fish

Notes: Interesting natural history information. This can include unique behaviors, remarkable features, sporting and table quality, details on migrations, seasonal patterns, or population trends.

Description: brownish-green back and sides with a white belly; long, stout body; rounded tail; continuous dorsal fin; bony plates covering head; males have a large "eye" spot at the base of the tail

Similar Species: Burbot (pg. 38)

Bowfin	Burbot	Bowfin	Burbot

| no barbel on chin | small barbel on chin | one dorsal fin, short anal fin | two dorsals, long anal fin |

BOWFIN
Amia calva

Other Names: dogfish, grindle or grinnel, mudfish, cypress trout, lake lawyer, beaverfish

Habitat: deep waters associated with vegetation in warm water lakes and rivers; feeds in shallow weedbeds

Range: the Mississippi River drainage east through the St. Lawrence drainage, south from Texas to Florida; Michigan—common throughout the Lower Peninsula

Food: fish, crayfish

Reproduction: In spring when water exceeds 61 degrees, the male removes vegetation to build a 2-foot-wide nest in sand or gravel; one or more females deposit up to 5,000 eggs in the nest; the male tenaciously guards the nest and "ball" of young.

Record and Average Size: Michigan state record—14 lb., 35 in.; Average size—2 to 5 lb. and 12 to 24 in.

Fishing ⬤ Tip: Fish large plugs and live bait along weed beds close to deep water at night.

Notes: A voracious predator, the Bowfin prowls shallow weed beds preying on anything that moves. Once thought detrimental to game fish populations, it is now considered an asset in controlling rough fish and stunted game fish. An air breather that tolerates low oxygen levels, Bowfin can survive short periods buried in mud.

Description: black to olive-green back; sides yellowish green; belly creamy white to yellow; light bar at base of tail; barbels around mouth are dark at base; adipose fin; lacks scales; round tail; anal fin 17-21 rays

Similar Species: Brown Bullhead (pg. 28), Yellow Bullhead (pg. 30), Flathead Catfish (pg. 34), Madtom/Stonecat (pg. 36)

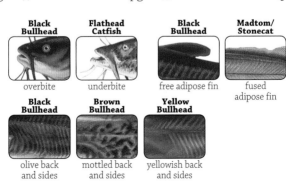

Black Bullhead — overbite

Flathead Catfish — underbite

Black Bullhead — free adipose fin

Madtom/Stonecat — fused adipose fin

Black Bullhead — olive back and sides

Brown Bullhead — mottled back and sides

Yellow Bullhead — yellowish back and sides

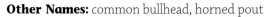

BLACK BULLHEAD
Ameiurus melas

Ictaluridae

Other Names: common bullhead, horned pout

Habitat: shallow, slow-moving streams and backwaters; lakes and ponds, tolerates extremely turbid conditions

Range: Southern Canada through the Great Lakes and the Mississippi River watershed to the Southwest and into Mexico; Michigan— statewide

Food: a scavenging opportunist; animal material (dead or alive), some plant matter

Reproduction: It spawns from late April to early June; builds a nest in shallow water with a muddy bottom; both sexes guard nest, eggs, and young till they are 1 inch long.

Record and Average Size: Michigan Record—3.44 lb., 17 in.; Average Size—4 to 16 oz., 8 to 10 in.

Fishing ⬭ Tip: In still water, fish the bottom with worms or cut bait.

Notes: The Black Bullhead is the most abundant of the three bullhead species found in Michigan, and on average the smallest. However, in 1987 the North American record was set in Michigan with an 8-lb. lunker; that record was sur-passed in 2015 by an 8 lb., 2 oz. giant caught in New York. It is more common to find large numbers of stunted Black Bullheads overpopulating a pond than it is to catch one large enough to keep.

Description: yellowish brown upper body, with mottling on back and sides; barbels around mouth; adipose fin; scaleless body; rounded tail; well-defined barbs on the pectoral spines: anal fin 22 to 23 rays

Similar Species: Black Bullhead (pg. 26), Yellow Bullhead (pg. 30), Flathead Catfish (pg. 34), Madtom/Stonecat (pg. 36)

Brown Bullhead	Black Bullhead	Madtom/ Stonecat	Brown Bullhead
free adipose fin	free adipose fin	fused adipose fin	overbite

Brown Bullhead	Black Bullhead	Yellow Bullhead	Flathead Catfish
mottled back and sides	olive back and sides	yellowish back and sides	underbite

BROWN BULLHEAD

Ameiurus nebulosus

Other Names: marbled or speckled bullhead, red cat

Habitat: warm, weedy lakes and sluggish streams

Range: Southern Canada through the Great Lakes down to the East Coast to Florida; introduced in the West; Michigan—statewide

Food: a scavenging opportunist; animal material (dead or alive), some plant matter

Reproduction: In early summer the male builds a nest in shallow water with good vegetation and a sandy or rocky bottom; both sexes guard the eggs and young.

Record and Average Size: Michigan Record—3.77 lb., 17.5 in.; Average Size—8 oz. to 2 lb., 8 to 12 in.

Fishing ⬭ Tip: Still fish on the bottom with worms or cut bait at night. The meat is red, firm, and very good when pan-fried.

Notes: The Brown Bullhead is the least common bullhead in Michigan. It can tolerate very turbid water but prefers clean, weedy lakes with soft bottoms. Young bullheads are black, and in early summer are often seen swimming in a tight, swarming ball. An adult fish may be seen guarding this ball of fry. This bullhead isn't highly pursued by anglers, though its reddish meat is tasty and fine table fare.

Description: olive head and back; yellowish-green head and sides; white belly; barbels on lower jaw are pale green or white; adipose fin; scaleless body; rounded tail; anal fin 24 to 27 rays

Similar Species: Black Bullhead (pg. 26), Brown Bullhead (pg. 28), Flathead Catfish (pg. 34), Madtom/Stonecat (pg. 36)

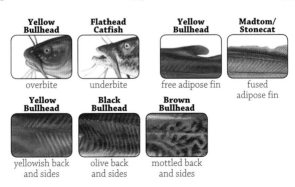

Yellow Bullhead	**Flathead Catfish**	**Yellow Bullhead**	**Madtom/ Stonecat**
overbite	underbite	free adipose fin	fused adipose fin

Yellow Bullhead	**Black Bullhead**	**Brown Bullhead**
yellowish back and sides	olive back and sides	mottled back and sides

YELLOW BULLHEAD
Ameiurus natalis

Ictaluridae

Other Names: white-whiskered bullhead, yellow cat

Habitat: well-vegetated, warm lakes and sluggish streams

Range: Southern Great Lakes through the eastern half of the US to the Gulf and into Mexico; introduced in the west; Michigan—statewide

Food: a scavenging opportunist, feeds on insects, crayfish, snails, small fish, and plant material

Reproduction: in late spring to early summer, males build nests in shallow water with some vegetation and a soft bottom; both sexes guard the eggs and young.

Record and Average Size: Michigan State Record—3.6 lb., 16.8 in.; Average size—½ to 1½ lb., 8 to 10 in.

Fishing ⬤ Tip: Still fish the lake bottom with worms or cut bait.

Notes: Yellow Bullheads are common in the inland lakes of Michigan but rare in the Great Lakes. The Yellow Bullhead is the bullhead species least tolerant of turbidity and prefers low-gradient streams, but will occupy reasonably clear lakes. Bullheads feed by "taste," locating food by following chemical trails through the water. This ability can be greatly diminished in polluted water, impairing their ability to find food. The Yellow Bullhead is less likely than other bullhead species to overpopulate a lake and become stunted.

Description: steel gray to silver on the back and sides; white belly; young fish have black spots on the sides; large fish lack spots and appear dark olive or slate gray; forked tail; adipose fin; long barbels around mouth; anal fin with rounded edge

Similar Species: Flathead Catfish (pg. 34), Bullheads (pp. 26–30)

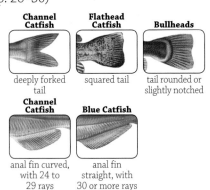

Channel Catfish	Flathead Catfish	Bullheads
deeply forked tail	squared tail	tail rounded or slightly notched

Channel Catfish	Blue Catfish
anal fin curved, with 24 to 29 rays	anal fin straight, with 30 or more rays

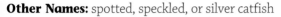

CHANNEL CATFISH
Ictalurus punctatus

Ictaluridae

Other Names: spotted, speckled, or silver catfish

Habitat: prefers clean, fast-moving streams with deep pools; stocked in many lakes; can tolerate turbid waters

Range: Southern Canada through the Midwest to the Gulf of Mexico into Mexico and Florida; introduced in most states; Michigan—Great Lakes drainages in the southern half of the state

Food: insects, crustaceans, fish, some plant debris

Reproduction: In early summer, the male builds a nest in a sheltered area, like undercut banks or behind logs; the male guards the eggs and young until the nest is deserted.

Record and Average Size: Michigan State Record—40 lb., 41.5 in.; Average Size—2 to 4 lb., 12 to 20 in.

Fishing ⬤ Tip: Drift live bait out of a riffle into a deep hole. During the day, fish brush piles with cut bait.

Notes: Though not highly respected by all northern Michigan anglers, Channel Catfish are hard fighters and considered fine table fare in southern Michigan. They were the first widely farmed food fish in the US and are now common in grocery stores and restaurants throughout the country. Many of the streams in southern Michigan have good populations of Channel Catfish.

Description: color variable, usually mottled yellow or brown;
belly cream to yellow; adipose fin; chin barbels; lacks scales;
tail squared; head broad and flattened; pronounced underbite

Similar Species: Channel Catfish (pg. 32), Bullheads
(pp. 26–30), Tadpole Madtom (pg. 36)

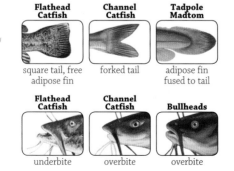

Flathead Catfish	**Channel Catfish**	**Tadpole Madtom**
square tail, free adipose fin	forked tail	adipose fin fused to tail
Flathead Catfish	**Channel Catfish**	**Bullheads**
underbite	overbite	overbite

FLATHEAD CATFISH
Pylodictis olivaris

Other Names: shovelnose, shovelhead; yellow, mud, pied or Mississippi cat

Habitat: deep pools of large rivers and impoundments

Range: the Mississippi River watershed into Mexico; large rivers in the Southwest; Michigan—a few rivers in Lake Michigan drainage

Food: fish, crayfish

Reproduction: It spawns when water reaches 65 to 80 degrees; the male builds and defends a nest in hollow logs, undercut banks, or other sheltered areas; large females may lay up to 30,000 eggs.

Record and Average Size: Michigan State Record—52 lb., 46 in.; Average Size—10 to 20 lb., 20 to 30 in.

Fishing ⬤ Tip: At night, fish large, active live bait in eddies at the mouth of small streams where they enter the main river.

Notes: The Flathead Catfish is a solitary predator that feeds aggressively on live fish. Flatheads spend the days hiding in bank holes and deep pools, then prowl log jams and the shallows for prey at night. Flatheads have been introduced into a few lakes in an attempt to control stunted panfish populations, with poor results. Flatheads are uncommon in Michigan but inhabit some large rivers, mostly in southern Michigan.

STONECAT

TADPOLE MADTOM

Description: Tadpole Madtom—dark olive to brown; dark line on side; large, fleshy head; Stonecat—similar but lacks dark lateral stripe, and has protruding upper jaw; both species have adipose fin continuous with tail

Similar Species: Bullheads (pp. 26–30), Catfish (pp. 32–34)

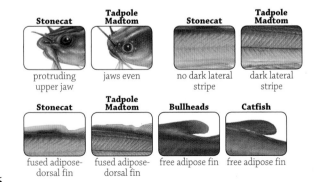

Stonecat	Tadpole Madtom	Stonecat	Tadpole Madtom
protruding upper jaw	jaws even	no dark lateral stripe	dark lateral stripe

Stonecat	Tadpole Madtom	Bullheads	Catfish
fused adipose-dorsal fin	fused adipose-dorsal fin	free adipose fin	free adipose fin

36

Ictaluridae

STONECAT *Noturus flavus*
TADPOLE MADTOM *Noturus gyrinus*

Other Names: willow cat

Habitat: weedy water near shore; under rocks in stream riffles

Range: eastern US; Michigan—southern Low Peninsula and Lakes Michigan, Erie, and Huron

Food: small invertebrates; algae and other plant matter

Reproduction: Both spawn in late spring; the female lays eggs under objects such as roots, rocks, logs, or in abandoned crayfish burrows; nest and eggs are guarded by one parent.

Record and Average Size: Michigan state record—none; Average Size—3 to 6 in.

Fishing ⬤ Tip: Reportedly, damaging the "slime" coating (by rolling them in sand) to make handling easier will reduce their effectiveness as bait.

Notes: Small, secretive nocturnal fish. Both species have venom glands at the base of the dorsal and pectoral fins. Though not lethal, the venom produces a painful burning sensation that can bring even the hardiest anglers to their knees. Both are effective baitfish.

Description: mottled brown with creamy chin and belly; eel-like body; small barbel at each nostril opening; longer barbel on chin; long dorsal fin similar to and just above anal fin

Similar Species: Bowfin (pg. 24), American Eel (pg. 42), Sea Lamprey (pg. 56)

Burbot	Bowfin	American Eel
two dorsals, long anal fin	one dorsal fin, short anal fin	fused dorsal, tail, and anal fin

Burbot	Bowfin	Sea Lamprey
small barbel on chin	no barbel on chin	mouth: sucking disk

BURBOT

Lota lota

Other Names: lawyer, eelpout, ling, cusk

Habitat: deep, cold, clear, rock-bottomed lakes and streams

Range: northern North America into Siberia and across northern Europe; Michigan—common in Lake Superior, Michigan, and Huron drainages of northern Michigan

Food: primarily small fish, fish eggs, clams, and crayfish

Reproduction: Pairs to large groups spawn together in mid-to-late winter under the ice over sand or gravel in less than 15 feet of water; after spawning, thrashing adults scatter fertilized eggs.

Record and Average Size: Michigan State Record—18.25 lb., 40 in.; Average Size—2 to 8 lb., 15 to 20 in.

Fishing Tip: Fish a white Marabou jig tipped with a minnow near the bottom.

Notes: The Burbot, a member of the Cod family, is a coldwater fish, seldom found in fisheries where the water temperature routinely exceeds 69 degrees. It is popular with ice anglers in some Western states and Scandinavia but considered a nuisance by most Michigan anglers. The flesh is firm, white, and good tasting, but not popular.

Description: gray back with purple or bronze reflections; silver sides; white underbelly; humped back; dorsal fin extends from hump to near tail; lateral line runs from head through the tail

Similar Species: White Bass (pg. 154)

Freshwater Drum	White Bass	Freshwater Drum	White Bass
triangular tail	forked tail	downturned mouth	upturned mouth

FRESHWATER DRUM

Aplodinotus grunniens

Other Names: sheepshead, croaker, thunderpumper, grinder, bubbler; commercially marketed as white perch

Habitat: slow to moderate current areas of rivers and streams; shallow lakes with soft bottoms; prefers clean water but tolerates some silt

Range: Canada south through the Midwest into eastern Mexico and to Guatemala; Michigan—rare inland, common in Lake Erie, Lake Michigan, and Lake St. Clair and their lower tributaries

Food: small fish, insects, crayfish, clams

Reproduction: In May and June, when water temperatures reach about 66 degrees, schools of drum lay eggs near the surface in open water, over sand or gravel; no parental care.

Record and Average Size: Michigan State Record—28.61 lb., 34 in.; Average Size—2 to 5 lb., 10 to 15 in.

Fishing ⬭ Tip: Fish small white or yellow jigs tipped with a crayfish tail just off the bottom.

Notes: The only freshwater member of a large family of marine fish, the Freshwater Drum gets its name from the grunting noise that males make, primarily to attract females. The sound is produced when specialized muscles rub along the swim bladder. The skull contains two enlarged L-shaped earstones called otoliths, which were once prized as jewelry by Native Americans. The flesh is flaky, white, and tasty but easily dries out when cooked.

Description: dark brown on top with yellow sides and white belly; long snake-like body with a large mouth; gill covers; a continuous dorsal, tail, and anal fin

Similar Species: Native Lampreys (pg. 54), Sea Lamprey (pg. 56)

American Eel

one gill cover, pectoral fins

Native Lampreys

seven gill slits, no pectoral fins

American Eel

mouth: jaws

Sea Lamprey

mouth: sucking disk

AMERICAN EEL
Anguilla rostrata

Other Names: common, Boston, Atlantic, or freshwater eel

Habitat: soft bottoms of medium to large streams, brackish tidewater along marine coasts

Range: the Atlantic Ocean; eastern and central North America; Central America; Michigan—uncommon but reported from all coastal drainages

Food: insects, crayfish, small fish

Reproduction: A "catadromous" species, it spends most of its life in freshwater, returning to the Sargasso Sea in the North Atlantic Ocean to spawn; females lay up to 20 million eggs; adults die after spawning.

Record and Average Size: Michigan State Record—7.44 lb., 43 in.; Average Size—2 to 3 lb., 20 to 30 in.

Fishing ⬭ Tip: At night, fish in backwaters just below dams by using nightcrawlers.

Notes: Leaf-shaped larval eels drift with ocean currents for about a year. When they reach the river mouths of North American and Central America, they morph into small eels (elvers). Males remain in the estuaries; females migrate upstream. At maturity (up to 20 years) adults return to the Sargasso Sea. Before settlement. eels commonly migrated up Great Lakes streams, but with all the dams present few make it now.

Description: olive to brown with dark spots along sides; long, cylindrical profile; single dorsal fin located just above the anal fin; body is encased in hard, plate-like scales; snout twice as long as head; needle-sharp teeth on both jaws

Similar Species: Spotted Gar (pg. 46)

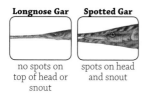

Longnose Gar	Spotted Gar
no spots on top of head or snout	spots on head and snout

LONGNOSE GAR

Lepisosteus osseus

Other Names: garfish

Habitat: quiet waters of larger rivers and lakes

Range: the central United States throughout the Mississippi River drainage south into Mexico, and a few rivers in the Great Lakes region; Michigan—common in all Lower Peninsula drainages

Food: minnows and other small fish

Reproduction: Females lay large, green eggs (which are toxic to mammals) in weedy shallows when water temperatures reach the high 60s; using a small disk on the snout, a newly hatched gar attaches to nearby plants, rocks, or branches until its digestive tract develops enough to begin feeding.

Record and Average Size: Michigan State Record—18 lb., 53 in.; Average Size—2 to 6 lb., 24 to 36 in.

Fishing ⬭ Tip: To consistently hook gar, you need to entangle their teeth; use spinner jigs made from frayed nylon line.

Notes: The Longnose Gar belongs to a prehistoric family of fish that can breathe air with the aid of a modified swim bladder. This adaptation makes them well suited to survive in increasingly polluted rivers and lakes. They hunt by floating motionless near the surface and then make a swift, sideways slash to capture prey. They prefer warm, deep water and often school near the surface. Gar are a valuable asset in controlling the increasing populations of rough fish.

Description: olive back and sides; spots on entire body, including snout, fins, and tail; cylindrical body; narrow snout slightly longer than head; sharp teeth on both jaws

Similar Species: Longnose Gar (pg. 44)

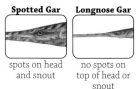

Spotted Gar	**Longnose Gar**
spots on head and snout	no spots on top of head or snout

SPOTTED GAR
Lepisosteus oculatus

Other Names: speckled gar

Habitat: quiet, clear, weedy water in streams and lakes

Range: southern Great Lakes basin southeast to Florida; Michigan—Lake Michigan drainages

Food: minnows, small fish

Reproduction: It spawns from May through June in quiet backwaters.

Record and Average Size: Michigan State Record—none; Average Size—2 to 6 lb. and 24 to 36 in.

Fishing Tip: To consistently hook gar, you need to entangle their teeth; use spinner jigs made from frayed nylon line.

Notes: The Spotted Gar is uncommon in Michigan and is on the decline. It requires cleaner, more weedy water than other gar species. Increased silt loads from runoff in Michigan streams have reduced the amount of suitable habitat. Like other gar, the Spotted Gar can gulp air and use its specialized swim bladder as a modified lung to breathe.

Description: slate-gray scaled body with black and brown spots; steep forehead with bulging eyes; front dorsal fin tinged green with a black spot; a single scallop-shaped dorsal fin

Similar Species: Mottled Sculpin (pg. 106)

Round Goby

scales on body

Mottled Sculpin

lacks scales

ROUND GOBY

Neogobius melanostomus

Other Names: rock goby

Habitat: rocky streams and lake shorelines; brackish coastal shorelines and tributary streams

Range: native to the Black and Caspian seas; invasive in northern Europe and the Great Lakes; Michigan—the Great Lakes

Food: mollusks, crustaceans, insects and fish eggs

Reproduction: It spawns several times a year in streams and along rocky shorelines; males protect the eggs.

Record and Average Size: Michigan State Record—none; Average Size—3 to 12 in.

Fishing ⬤ Tip: Check bait pails carefully to ensure that gobies are not introduced to new lakes.

Notes: The Round Goby is an aggressively expanding invasive species that negatively impacts native species. Where it becomes established, native fish populations decrease. Introduced to the Great Lakes in the late 1980s, they are now well established. Larger gobies are effective predators on Zebra Mussels, but their overall effect on lake ecology is negative.

Description: silvery with a blue to blue-green metallic shine on back, with silver sides, white belly; faint dark stripes along sides; dark spot behind the gill and directly above the pectoral fin; large mouth with a protruding lower jaw

Similar Species: Gizzard Shad (pg. 52), Mooneye (pg. 70)

Alewife	Gizzard Shad	Alewife	Mooneye

| anal fin typically 17 or 18 rays | anal fin typically 27 to 34 rays | scaled, saw-like keel | fleshy keel |

50

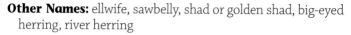

ALEWIFE

Alosa pseudoharengus

Other Names: ellwife, sawbelly, shad or golden shad, big-eyed herring, river herring

Habitat: open water of the Great Lakes and a few inland lakes

Range: the Atlantic Ocean from Labrador to Florida; St. Lawrence River drainage and the Great Lakes; Michigan— Lakes Superior, Michigan, and Huron

Food: zooplankton, filamentous algae

Reproduction: In the Great Lakes, spawning occurs in bays and along protected shorelines during early summer

Record and Average Size: Michigan state record—none; Average Size—4 to 8 in.

Fishing Tip: An alewife floated near the bottom close to shore is a good bait for Lake Trout in the spring.

Notes: The Alewife is an Atlantic herring that was accidentally introduced to the eastern Great Lakes; another invasive species, the Sea Lamprey, was introduced around the same time, decimating the populations of Lake Trout and other predator fish in the lakes. This left the Alewife with few predators, and its population numbers exploded. Eventually, scientists learned how to control Sea Lamprey populations, and fishing regulations helped predator fish populations rebound. The Alewife population soon crashed. Not well adapted to freshwater lakes, these fish are subject to frequent summer kills. Alewives were once commercially netted in the eastern Great Lakes and used for animal food.

51

Description: deep, laterally compressed body; silvery blue back with white sides and belly; young fish have a dark spot on shoulder behind the gill; small mouth; last rays of dorsal fin form a long thread

Similar Species: Alewife (pg. 50), Mooneye (pg. 70)

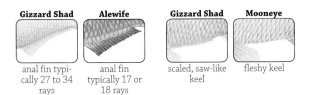

Gizzard Shad	Alewife		Gizzard Shad	Mooneye
anal fin typically 27 to 34 rays	anal fin typically 17 or 18 rays		scaled, saw-like keel	fleshy keel

Clupeidae

GIZZARD SHAD
Dorosoma cepedianum

Other Names: hickory, mud, or jack shad; skipjack

Habitat: large rivers, reservoirs, lakes, swamps, and temporarily flooded pools; brackish and saline waters in coastal areas

Range: the St. Lawrence River and the Great Lakes; the Mississippi, Atlantic, and Gulf Slope drainages from Quebec to Mexico, south to central Florida; Michigan—Lake Michigan, Lake Huron, and Lake Erie drainages

Food: herbivorous filter feeder

Reproduction: Spawning takes place in tributary streams and along lakeshores in early summer; schooling adults release eggs in open water without regard for individual mates.

Record and Average Size: Michigan State Record—4.12 lb., 21 in.; Average Size—1 to 8 oz., 4 to 8 in.

Fishing ⬤ Tip: Large Gizzard Shad can be caught by using waxworms in quiet pools at the current's edge.

Notes: The Gizzard Shad is a widespread, prolific fish that is best known as forage for popular game fish. At times Gizzard Shad can become overabundant and experience large die-offs. The name "gizzard" refers to this shad's long, convoluted intestine that is often packed with sand. Though Gizzard Shad are a management problem at times, they form a valuable link in turning plankton into usable forage for large game fish.

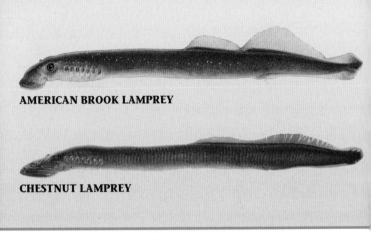

AMERICAN BROOK LAMPREY

CHESTNUT LAMPREY

Description: eel-like body with round, toothed, suction-cup-like mouth and seven paired gill openings; dorsal fin is long extending to the tail; no paired fins

Similar Species: Sea Lamprey (pg. 56) American Eel (pg. 42)

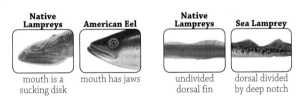

Native Lampreys	American Eel	Native Lampreys	Sea Lamprey
mouth is a sucking disk	mouth has jaws	undivided dorsal fin	dorsal divided by deep notch

NATIVE LAMPREYS
Ichthyomyzon, Lampetra

Other Names: Silver, Chestnut, American Brook, and Northern Brook Lamprey

Habitat: Juveniles live in the quiet pools of streams and rivers; adults may move into some lakes.

Range: freshwater of eastern North America; Michigan—Silver, Northern, and American Brook Lampreys found throughout state, Chestnut Lamprey restricted to Lower Peninsula

Food: Juvenile lampreys are filter feeders in stream bottoms; adults are either parasitic on fish or do not feed.

Reproduction: Adults build nests in the gravel of streambeds, typically after water temperatures reach about 55 degrees, then die shortly after spawning.

Records and Average Size: Michigan State Record—none; Average Size—6 to 12 in.

Fishing ⬤ Tip: Not targeted or used for bait by anglers

Notes: There are four native lampreys in Michigan. Adult Chestnut and Silver Lampreys are parasitic, often leaving small, round wounds on their prey. The American Brook Lamprey and Northern Brook Lamprey are not parasitic and do not feed as adults. Michigan lampreys coexist with other native fish species with little or no effect on populations. The lampreys are some of Earth's oldest vertebrates, with fossil records dating back 500 million years.

Description: eel-like body; round, toothy, suction-cup-like mouth; seven paired gill openings; dorsal fin extends to the tail and is divided into two sections by a deep notch; no paired fins

Similar Species: Native Lampreys (pg. 54), American Eel (pg. 42)

Sea Lamprey	American Eel	Sea Lamprey	Native Lampreys
mouth is a sucking disk	mouth has jaws	dorsal divided by deep notch	undivided dorsal fin

SEA LAMPREY
Petromyzon marinus

Other Names: landlocked or lake lamprey

Habitat: Juveniles live in quiet pools of freshwater streams; adults are free-swimming in lakes or oceans.

Range: Atlantic Ocean from Greenland to Florida, Norway to the Mediterranean; the Great Lakes; Michigan—Lakes Superior, Michigan, and Huron, some tributaries of each

Food: juveniles are filter feeders in the bottoms of streams; adult is parasitic on fish, attaching itself using disc-shaped sucker mouth, then using its sharp tongue to rasp through the fish's scales and skin to feed on blood and bodily fluids

Reproduction: Both adults build a nest in the gravel of a clear stream, then die shortly after spawning; the young remain in the stream several years before returning to the lake as adults.

Record and Average Size: Michigan State Record—none; Average Size—12 to 24 in.

Fishing ⬤ Tip: Do not return Sea Lampreys to the lake.

Notes: Native to the Atlantic Ocean, the Sea Lamprey entered the Great Lakes via the St. Lawrence Seaway. It was initially blocked by Niagara Falls, but when the Welland Canal allowed it to bypass the falls, it entered the upper Great Lakes. The first specimen was found in Lake Superior in 1936; soon after, Lake Trout and Whitefish populations declined. Control measures, including traps and chemicals, have reduced Sea Lamprey numbers, allowing native fish populations to slowly recover.

BIGHEAD CARP

SILVER CARP

Description: dark gray to black back; silver-gray sides with dark blotches; low-set eyes; upturned mouth; tiny body scales, none on head

Similar Species: Common Carp (pg. 60)

Bighead Carp
small silver scales

Silver Carp
small silver scales

Common Carp
large, yellow scales with a dark margin

Bighead Carp
keeled belly from pelvic fin to anal fin

Silver Carp
keeled belly from gills to anal fin

Bighead/Silver Carp
eyes low on head

Common Carp
eyes high on head

58

BIGHEAD CARP *Hypophthalmichthys nobilis*
SILVER CARP *Hypophthalmichthys molitrix*

Cyprinidae

Other Names: river carp, lake fish, speckled amur, shiner carp

Habitat: large, warm rivers and connected lakes

Range: Asia; introduced in other parts of the world; Michigan—approaching Lake Michigan and a few southern Michigan streams

Food: aquatic vegetation and floating plankton, mostly algae

Reproduction: It spawns from late spring to early summer in warm, flowing water.

Record and Average Size: Michigan State Record—none; Average Size—5 to 50 lb., 15 to 36 in.

Fishing Tip: As filter feeders, Bighead Carp and Silver Carp are targets for bow fishermen but not often for anglers. Reportedly they can be caught with wet flies.

Notes: Bighead Carp are the fourth-most important aquaculture fish in the world. They were introduced to the US to control algae in southern aquaculture ponds and escaped to the Mississippi River. At this time these carp are not established in Michigan, but they may soon be. The Silver Carp, and to a lesser degree the Bighead Carp, makes high leaps from the water when frightened by boats. There is concern that Bighead Carp, if established in Michigan, could cause great harm to the state's fisheries.

Description: brassy yellow to dark-olive back and sides; whitish-yellow belly; round mouth has two pairs of barbels; reddish tail and anal fin; each scale has a dark margin

Similar Species: Bighead Carp (pg. 58), Silver Carp (pg. 58)

Common Carp

large yellow scales with dark margin

Bighead/Silver Carp

small silver scales

Common Carp

eyes high on head

Bighead/Silver Carp

eyes low on head

COMMON CARP

Cyprinus carpio

Other Names: German, European, mirror, or leather carp; buglemouth

Habitat: warm, shallow, quiet, well-vegetated waters of streams and lakes

Range: native to Asia; introduced throughout the world; Michigan—statewide

Food: opportunistic feeder; prefers insect larvae, crustaceans and mollusks, but at times eats algae and some higher plants

Reproduction: It spawns from late spring to early summer in very shallow water at stream and lake edges; it's very obvious when spawning, with a great deal of splashing.

Record and Average Size: Michigan State Record—61.5 lb., 47.5 in.; Average Size—3 to 15 lb., 18 to 24 in.

Fishing ⬤ Tip: Fish amid shallow vegetation at night for the biggest carp.

Notes: The Common Carp is one of the world's most important freshwater fish. This fast-growing fish provides sport and food for millions of people throughout its range. This Asian minnow was introduced into Europe in the twelfth century but didn't make it to North America until the nineteenth century. Carp are a highly prized sport fish in Europe, but they have not gained the same status in the US, even though some line and bow anglers enthusiastically fish for them.

Description: gray to olive brown, often with a dark stripe on side and black spot at the base of tail; red spot behind eye; breeding males develop horn-like tubercles on the head

Similar Species: Fathead Minnow (pg. 66), Creek Chub

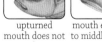

Hornyhead Chub	**Fathead Minnow**	**Creek Chub**
downturned mouth extends to eye	upturned mouth does not extend to eye	mouth extends to middle of eye

HORNYHEAD CHUB

Nocomis biguttatus

Cyprinidae

Other Names: redtail, horned, or river chub

Habitat: small to medium-size streams; occasionally found in lakes near stream mouths

Range: the northern Midwest through the Great Lakes region; Michigan—common in the Lower Peninsula and western Upper Peninsula; rare in the eastern U.P.

Food: small aquatic invertebrates, zooplankton

Reproduction: In late spring the male excavates a 1- to 3-foot-diameter pit in a gravelly stream riffle, then fills it with small stones, creating a 6- to 8-inch-high mound; females lay eggs on the mound; the male covers fertilized eggs with gravel; other species such as Common Shiner may also use the mound for spawning.

Record and Average Size: Michigan State Record—none; Average Size—4 to 12 in.

Fishing Tip: Chubs are an excellent baitfish, but not very hardy.

Notes: Michigan's six chubs (Creek, Hornyhead, Gravel, Lake, Silver, and Speckled) are our largest native minnows. The Creek and Hornyhead grow to a foot long and can be caught with hook and line. The Hornyhead is a common bait minnow and is often called the Redtail Chub. Due to high demand, anglers sometimes pay over a dollar per fish, making it costlier per pound than lobster. Recently, habitat loss and harvest pressure by bait dealers have caused populations to decline.

Description: moderately dark back; two broad lateral bands on tan background; in breeding males the tan turns orange and the belly becomes bright red or orange; blunt nose

Similar Species: Southern Redbelly Dace, Finescale Dace

Northern Redbelly Dace

curved mouth, lower jaw slightly ahead of upper

Southern Redbelly Dace

straight mouth, upper jaw slightly ahead of the lower

Northern Redbelly Dace

two dark lateral stripes

Finescale Dace

single dark lateral stripe

NORTHERN REDBELLY DACE

Phoxinus eos

Other Names: redbelly, leatherback, yellow-belly dace

Habitat: small streams and bog lakes

Range: Northwest Territories to Hudson Bay, northeastern US, and eastern Canada; Michigan—common in most of Michigan, but absent from the southernmost streams

Food: plant material

Reproduction: From May to early August, a single female accompanied by several males will dart among masses of filamentous algae, laying 5 to 30 non-adhesive eggs at a time; males fertilize the eggs, which hatch in 8 to 10 days with no parental care.

Record and Average Size: Michigan state record—none; Average Size—2 to 3 in.

Fishing ⬤ Tip: Dace are average as bait minnows. They survive in the bait pail pretty well but not long once on the hook.

Notes: There are seven species of minnows in Michigan that are referred to as daces. These small fish live in a variety of habitats. The Northern Redbelly Dace is a hardy fish often found in the acidic water of bogs, stained lakes, and beaver ponds, as well as small clear streams. Breeding males are one of Michigan's brightest colored fish and surpass many aquarium fish in beauty. Northern Redbelly Dace often hybridize with other species and sometimes form all-female populations.

65

NON-SPAWNING ADULT

SPAWNING MALE

Description: olive back, golden yellow sides, and white belly; dark lateral line widens to spot at base of tail; rounded snout and fins; no scales on head; dark blotch on dorsal fin

Similar Species: Hornyhead Chub (pg. 62), Creek Chub

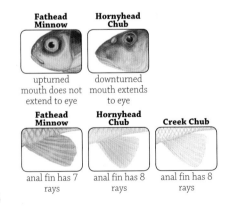

Fathead Minnow

upturned mouth does not extend to eye

Hornyhead Chub

downturned mouth extends to eye

Fathead Minnow

anal fin has 7 rays

Hornyhead Chub

anal fin has 8 rays

Creek Chub

anal fin has 8 rays

FATHEAD MINNOW
Pimephales promelas

Other Names: fathead, blackhead, tuffy, mudminnow

Habitat: streams, ponds, and lakes; particularly shallow, weedy, or turbid areas lacking predators

Range: east of the Rocky Mountains in the US and Canada; Michigan—statewide

Food: primarily herbivorous, but will eat insects and copepods

Reproduction: From the time water temperatures reach 60 degrees in spring through August, the male prepares a nest under rocks and sticks; the female enters, turns upside down, and lays adhesive eggs; after the female leaves, the male fertilizes the eggs, which it then guards, fans with its fins, and massages with a special, mucus-like pad on its back.

Record and Average Size: Michigan State Record—none; Average Size—1 to 2 in.

Fishing Tip: Some anglers report catching fewer fish when using breeding male Fatheads, perhaps due to their color or differing scent.

Notes: Minnows are small fish; they are not the young of larger species. The Fathead is one of our most numerous and widespread fish in Michigan, and it is commonly used as bait. It is hardy and withstands extremely low oxygen levels—both in the wild and in bait buckets. Prior to spawning, the male develops a dark coloration, breeding tubercles on its head that resemble small horns, and a mucus-like patch on its back.

67

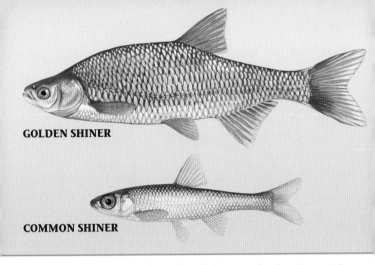

GOLDEN SHINER

COMMON SHINER

Description: silver body with a dark green back, often with a dark body stripe; breeding males have bluish heads and rosy pink body and fins

Similar Species: Hornyhead Chub, Golden Shiner

Common Shiner	**Golden Shiner**	**Common Shiner**	**Hornyhead Chub**
8 to 10 rays on anal fin (usually 9)	11 to 15 rays on anal fin	eye large in relation to the head	eye small in relation to head

COMMON SHINER

Luxilus cornutus

Cyprinidae

Other Names: common, eastern, creek, or redfin shiner

Habitat: lakes, rivers, and streams; most common in pools of streams and small rivers

Range: the Midwest through eastern US and Canada; Michigan—statewide

Food: small insects, algae, zooplankton

Reproduction: beginning in late May, the male prepares a nest of small stones and gravel at the head of a stream riffle; females are courted with great flourish.

Record and Average Size: Michigan State Record—none; Average Size—3 to 12 in.

Fishing Tip: Large Common Shiners can be caught on dry flies and are occasionally eaten; though not as meaty as panfish, they are every bit as tenacious when hooked.

Notes: There are just under 20 minnow species in Michigan known as shiners, and many of them are very hard to tell apart. Not all shiners are as flashy as the name indicates. Some are dull-colored and show almost no silver on the sides. The Common Shiner is one of the larger native Michigan minnows, occasionally reaching 12 inches in length. It has now replaced the Golden Shiner as the common bait shiner, though it is somewhat less hardy on the hook.

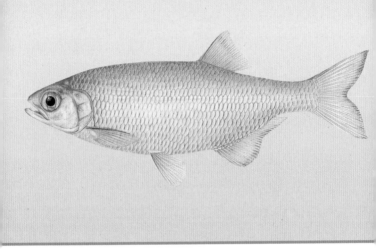

Description: dark green to dark blue back and upper sides; bright silver or golden sides; large yellow-tinged eye; large scales; thin body flattened from side to side with a sharp scale ridge (keel) from throat to pelvic fin, forward-facing mouth with small teeth

Similar Species: Gizzard Shad (pg. 52)

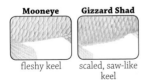

Mooneye	Gizzard Shad
fleshy keel	scaled, saw-like keel

MOONEYE
Hiodon tergisus

Other Names: white shad, slicker, toothed herring, river whitefish

Habitat: clear, quiet waters of large lakes and the backwaters of large streams

Range: Hudson Bay drainage east to the St. Lawrence drainage, through the Mississippi drainage south into Arkansas and Alabama; Michigan—Lake St. Clair and St. Clair River

Food: insects, small fish, crayfish, snails

Reproduction: Spawning takes place in turbid pools and backwaters when water temperatures reach the mid 50s.

Record and Average Size: Michigan State Record—1.69 lb., 14.38 in.; Average Size 12 to 16 oz., 10 to 12 in.

Fishing ⬤ Tip: Mooneyes will take flies, but they are not great fighters.

Notes: The Mooneye is a flashy fish that jumps repeatedly when hooked. However, it is bony, with little meat except along the back. It commonly feeds on insects at or near the surface in slackwater of large lakes and rivers. The very similar looking Goldeye is found in other Great Lake States but not Michigan. Though small, it is related to the South American Arapaima, the world's largest scaled freshwater fish.

IOWA DARTER

JOHNNY DARTER

Description: Iowa Darter—brown back with faint blotches; sides have 9 to 12 vertical bars; dark spot under eye; bars are more pronounced and colors brighter in breeding males; Johnny Darter—tan to olive back and upper sides with dark blotches and speckling; sides tan to golden with X, Y, and W patterns; breeding males dark with black bars

Similar Species: Iowa Darter; Johnny Darter

Iowa Darter **Johnny Darter**

blotches or bars on sides   X, Y and W markings on sides

IOWA DARTER *Etheostoma exile*
JOHNNY DARTER *Etheostoma nigrum*

Other Names: red-sided, yellowbelly, or weed darter

Habitat: Iowa Darters inhabit slow-flowing streams and lakes that have some vegetation or an algae mat; Johnny Darters are found in most rivers, streams, and lakes

Range: Rocky Mountains east across Canada and the US through the Great Lakes region; Michigan—both are found statewide

Food: waterfleas, insect larvae

Reproduction: In May and June, males migrate to shorelines to establish breeding areas; females move from territory to territory, spawning with several males; each sequence produces 7 to 10 eggs, which sink and attach to the bottom.

Record and Average Size: Michigan State Record—none; Average Size—2 to 4 in.

Fishing Tip: Not hardy enough to be a good bait minnow

Notes: Relatives of Yellow Perch and Walleye, darters are primarily stream fish that live among rocks in fast currents. Small swim bladders allow them to sink rapidly to the bottom after making a quick "dart," thus avoiding being swept away by the current. The Johnny is the most common darter and is found in most lakes, streams, and rivers statewide. The Iowa Darter is a lake species that inhabits weedy shorelines. They are hard to see when still, but easy to spot when making a quick dart to a new resting place, where they perch on their pectoral fins.

Description: olive or golden brown back; large continuous spiny dorsal fin; spots between dorsal spines; large spine on pelvic fins; scaleless head

Similar Species: Yellow Perch (pg. 80); Trout-perch (pg. 158)

Ruffe	**Yellow Perch**	**Trout-Perch**
continuous dorsal fin, spots between rays	separated dorsal fin, no spots	single dorsal fin, no spots

RUFFE

Gymnocephalus cernuus

Other Names: blacktail, pope, redfin darter, river ruffe

Habitat: bottom-dweller of lakes and streams down to about 300 feet

Range: temperate regions of Europe and Asia; western Great Lakes; Michigan—the Great Lakes

Food: mostly insect larvae

Reproduction: It spawns April through June in rocky shallows; it's an aggressive breeder that displaces native fish; may have two broods per year.

Record and Average Size: Michigan State Record—none; Average Size—3 to 10 in.

Fishing ⬭ Tip: Ruffes should never be used as bait and care should be taken to not spread them to other lakes or streams.

Notes: The Ruffe is a very aggressively invasive species that was introduced to the Great Lakes from ship ballast in the 1980s. Where it is established as invasive in Europe and the US, native fish populations are in decline. Notify the DNR if Ruffe are found anywhere far from any of the Great Lakes and tributary streams.

SAUGER

SAUGEYE

Description: slender body; gray to dark silver or yellowish brown with dark blotches on sides; black spots on spiny dorsal fin; may exhibit some white on lower margin of tail, but lacks prominent white spot found on Walleyes

Similar Species: Walleye (pg. 78), Saugeye (Walleye Sauger hybrid)

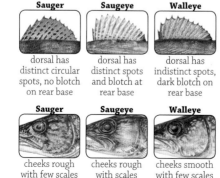

Sauger	Saugeye	Walleye
dorsal has distinct circular spots, no blotch on rear base	dorsal has distinct spots and blotch at rear base	dorsal has indistinct spots, dark blotch on rear base

Sauger	Saugeye	Walleye
cheeks rough with few scales	cheeks rough with scales	cheeks smooth with few scales

SAUGER
Sander canadensis

Other Names: sand pike, spotfin pike, river pike, jackfish, jack salmon

Habitat: large lakes and rivers

Range: Canada and the northern US; the Mississippi, Missouri, Ohio, and Tennessee River drainages; Michigan—historically in Lakes Superior, Michigan, Erie, and Huron, now common only in St. Clair River and Lake St. Clair

Food: small fish, aquatic insects, crayfish

Reproduction: It spawns in April and May as water approaches 50 degrees; adults move into the shallow waters of tributaries and headwaters to randomly deposit eggs over gravel beds.

Record and Average Size: Michigan State Record— 6.56 lb., 25.5 in.; Average Size—8 oz. to 2 lb., 10 to 15 in.

Fishing ⬤ Tip: Saugers are slightly more aggressive daytime feeders compared to Walleyes and respond to a little faster retrieval and brighter colors during summer river fishing.

Notes: Though the Sauger is the Walleye's smaller cousin, it is a big-water fish primarily found in large lakes and rivers. It is slow-growing, often reaching only 2 pounds in 20 years. Saugers were never common in Michigan but have declined greatly in the last 20 years. They are still common in other parts of the Great Lakes region and the upper Mississippi River. A Saugeye is a natural hybrid of Walleye and Sauger and rare in Michigan.

Description: long, round body; dark silver or golden to dark olive brown in color; spines in both first dorsal and anal fin; sharp canine teeth; dark spot at base of the three last spines in the dorsal fin; white spot on bottom lobe of tail

Similar Species: Sauger (pg. 76), Saugeye (Walleye-Sauger hybrid)

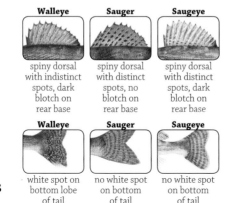

Walleye	Sauger	Saugeye
spiny dorsal with indistinct spots, dark blotch on rear base	spiny dorsal with distinct spots, no blotch on rear base	spiny dorsal with distinct spots, dark blotch on rear base

Walleye	Sauger	Saugeye
white spot on bottom lobe of tail	no white spot on bottom of tail	no white spot on bottom of tail

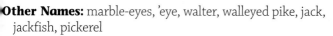

WALLEYE
Sander vitreus

Other Names: marble-eyes, 'eye, walter, walleyed pike, jack, jackfish, pickerel

Habitat: lakes and streams, abundant in some very large lakes

Range: northern states and Canada, now widely stocked in the US; Michigan—common statewide except the southwest

Food: mainly small fish, but also eats insects, crayfish, leeches, and frogs

Reproduction: Spawning takes place in tributary streams or rocky lake shoals when spring water temperatures reach 45 to 50 degrees; no parental care is given.

Records and Average Size: Michigan State Record—17.19 lb., 36.8 inches; Average Size—1 to 3 lb., 10 to 18 in.

Fishing ⬯ Tip: Fishing jigs that simulate Madtoms on rocky shorelines at night can be very effective for large Walleye.

Notes: Walleyes are Michigan's most popular sport fish. A dogged opponent, but not a spectacular fighter or jumper, the Walleye is at the top of the list of North American fish when it reaches the table. A reflective layer of pigment in the eye (tapetum lucidum) allows Walleyes and Saugers to see well in low-light conditions. As a result, Walleyes are most active at dusk, dawn, night, and under light-reducing conditions such as choppy waves and cloudy skies.

Description: 6 to 9 dark, vertical bars on bright yellowish green to orange background; long dorsal fin with two distinct lobes; lower fins have a yellow to orange tinge

Similar Species: Trout-Perch (pg. 158), Walleye (pg. 78)

Yellow Perch	Trout-Perch	Yellow Perch	Walleye

| no adipose fin | adipose fin | lacks prominent white spot on tail | prominent white spot on tail |

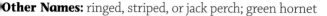

Percidae

YELLOW PERCH
Perca flavescens

Other Names: ringed, striped, or jack perch; green hornet

Habitat: lakes and streams; prefers clear, open water

Range: northern US and southern Canada; Michigan—statewide

Food: small fish, insects, snails, leeches, and crayfish

Reproduction: It spawns at night in shallow, weedy areas soon after ice-out when water warms to 45 degrees; the female drapes gelatinous ribbons of eggs over submerged vegetation.

Record and Average Size: Michigan State Record—3.74 lb., 21 in.; Average Size—6 to 10 oz., 6 to 10 in.

Fishing Tip: Perch are very sensitive to color, so when fishing is slow, consider changing jig color.

Notes: Yellow Perch are very common in Michigan and possibly the most important food and sport fish in the state. Perch travel in schools of about the same age class and size. Perch are an important link in the food web, serving as forage for larger sport fish. In turn, overfishing of these top predators can lead to a population of "stunted" or undersized perch. Yellow Perch reproduction in the Great Lakes seems to be adversely affected by high Alewife populations. The perch population quickly recovers in years that the Alewife population crashes.

Description: olive-green to yellow-brown with wavy bars on the sides; distinct dark teardrop below the eye

Similar Species: Northern Pike (pg. 86), Muskellunge (pg. 84)

Grass Pickerel	**Northern Pike**
gill cover fully scaled	lower half of gill cover unscaled

Grass Pickerel	**Northern Pike**
dark teardrop under the eye	lacks dark teardrop

Grass Pickerel	**Muskellunge**
rounded tail	pointed tail

GRASS PICKEREL
Esox americanus

Other Names: grass or mud pike, mud or little pickerel

Habitat: shallow, weedy lakes and sluggish streams

Range: eastern one-third of the US from the Great Lakes basin to Maine, south to Florida; Michigan—southern half of Lower Peninsula

Food: small fish, aquatic insects

Reproduction: Spawning takes place in April and May just as the ice goes out; eggs are laid in shallow weed beds.

Record and Average Size: Michigan state record—none; Average Size—8 to 12 oz., 8 to 12 in.

Fishing ⬤ Tip: Use a fly rod to fish the outside edge of weed beds with a streamer.

Notes: The Grass Pickerel is very common in some southern Michigan lakes but is too small to be either a panfish or a game fish. Anglers catching Grass Pickerel often think they've caught small Northern Pike and return them to the water to "grow up." It is unclear what relationship there is between Grass Pickerel and Northern Pike. In some lakes they coexist, while in others there is just one or the other.

MUSKELLUNGE

TIGER MUSKIE

Description: torpedo-shaped body; dorsal fin near tail; sides typically silver to silver-green with dark spots or bars on light background; pointed lobes on tail and paired fins; lower half of gill cover has no scales

Similar Species: Northern Pike (pg. 86), Tiger Muskie

Muskellunge

dark marks on light background

Northern Pike

light marks on dark background

Muskellunge

6 or more pores on each side under the jaw

Northern Pike

5 or fewer pores each side under the jaw

Muskellunge

pointed tail

Northern Pike

rounded tail

Tiger Muskie

rounded tail

MUSKELLUNGE
Esox masquinongy

Other Names: musky, muskie, 'ski, lunge

Habitat: large, clear lakes with extensive weedbeds; medium to large rivers with slow currents and deep pools

Range: the Great Lakes east to Maine, south through the Ohio River drainage to Tennessee; Michigan—central and northern Michigan

Food: small fish; occasionally muskrats, ducklings

Reproduction: It spawns mid-April to May when water temperatures reach 50 to 60 degrees; eggs are laid in dead vegetation in tributaries, or in shallow bays with muck bottoms; the male and female swim side by side for several hundred yards, depositing fertilized eggs.

Record and Average Size: Michigan State Record—58 lb., 59 in.; Average Size—10 to 20 lb., 30 to 40 in.

Fishing Tip: Fish medium-size suckers under a bobber in open holes in large weed beds.

Notes: Muskies are legendary among anglers for their sheer size, power, and explosive strikes. They are thinly dispersed, typically with only one fish every 2 to 3 acres. They prefer shallow lakes and slow-moving streams but occasionally show up in deep, rocky lakes with just a few weed beds. Muskies hybridize with Northern Pike to produce the Tiger Muskellunge. Because they are less aggressive in rearing tanks, Tiger Muskies are commonly used for stocking lakes.

Description: long body with dorsal fin near tail; head is long and flattened in front, forming a duck-like snout; dark green back, light green sides with bean-shaped light spots; Silver Pike are a rare, silver colored mutation of Northern Pike

Similar Species: Muskellunge (pg. 84), Tiger Muskie (pg. 84)

light marks on dark background
(Northern Pike)

dark marks on light background
(Muskellunge)

(Northern Pike / Muskellunge)

5 or fewer pores each side under the jaw (Northern Pike)

6 or more pores on each side under the jaw (Muskellunge)

Northern Pike — rounded tail

Muskellunge — pointed tail

Tiger Muskie — rounded tail

NORTHERN PIKE

Esox lucius

Other Names: pickerel, jack, gator, hammerhandle, snot rocket

Habitat: lakes, ponds, streams, and rivers; often found near weeds; small pike tolerate water temperatures up to 70 degrees, but larger fish prefer cooler water, 55 degrees or less

Range: Northern Europe, Asia, and North America; Michigan—statewide

Food: small fish, occasionally frogs, and crayfish

Reproduction: In late March to early April in tributaries and marshes when water reaches 34 to 40 degrees; attended by 1 to 3 males, the female deposits eggs in shallow vegetation.

Records and Average Size: Michigan Record—39 lb., 51.5 in.; Average Size—2 to 10 lb., 24 to 30 in.

Fishing ⬤ Tip: Floating dead sucker minnows, near the bottom, in weedy shallows during the first couple of weeks of the fishing season is deadly for big pike.

Notes: Michigan's most widespread game fish. Good table quality but bony. These intramuscular bones and slimy coating are adaptations for quick bursts of speed. A daytime ambush hunter, Northerns often lie in wait in weedy cover capturing prey with a fast lunge. That sudden burst of speed is also good for breaking lines just at the boat.

Description: back is olive, blue-gray to black with wormlike markings; sides bronze to olive with red spots tinged light brown; lower fins red-orange with white leading edge; tail squared or slightly forked

Similar Species: Brown Trout (pg. 90), Rainbow Trout (pg. 94), Lake Trout (pg. 92), Splake

Brook Trout	**Brown Trout**	**Rainbow Trout**	**Lake Trout**
worm-like marks, red spots	large dark spots, small red dots	pink stripe on silver body	sides lack red spots

Brook Trout	**Lake Trout**	**Splake**
tail square to slightly forked	tail deeply forked	tail moderately forked

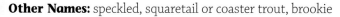

BROOK TROUT
Salvelinus fontinalis

Salmonidae

Other Names: speckled, squaretail or coaster trout, brookie

Habitat: cool, clear streams and small lakes with sand or gravel bottoms and moderate vegetation; coastal in large lakes; prefers water temperatures of 50 to 60 degrees or below

Range: Great Lakes region north to Labrador, south through the Appalachians to Georgia; introduced into the western US, Canada, Europe, and South America; Michigan—statewide

Food: insects, small fish, leeches, crustaceans

Reproduction: It spawns in late fall at 40- to 49-degree water temperatures on gravel bars in stream riffles and in lakes where springs aerate eggs; the female builds a 12-inch-deep nest in gravel, then buries fertilized eggs. Males may guard the nest during construction.

Records and Average Size: Michigan State Record—9.5 lb., 28.1 in.; Average Size—8 to 16 oz., 8 to 10 in.

Fishing ⬤ Tip: For big Brook Trout "coasters," fish the mouth of Great Lake streams in the evening with brown or green poppers.

Notes: Michigan's state fish, the Brook Trout requires cold clear water no warmer than the mid 50s. Brookies are prized by trout fishermen for their voracious appetite, strong runs, and delicate flavor. With stocking, Michigan state supports a stable Brook Trout fishery, but it is susceptible to stream degradation and climate changes, particularly warming waters.

89

BROWN TROUT

TIGER TROUT

Description: golden brown to olive back and sides; large dark spots on sides, dorsal fin, and sometimes upper lobe of tail; red spots with light halos scattered along sides

Similar Species: Rainbow Trout (pg. 94), Lake Trout (pg. 92), Brook Trout (pg. 88), Tiger Trout

Brown Trout	**Rainbow Trout**	**Lake Trout**
dark spots on brown or olive	pink stripe on silvery body	white spots on dark background

Brown Trout	**Brook Trout**	**Tiger Trout**
lacks worm-like markings	worm-like markings on back	worm-like markings on back and sides

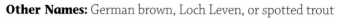

BROWN TROUT

Salmo trutta

Other Names: German brown, Loch Leven, or spotted trout

Habitat: open ocean near its spawning streams and clear, cold, gravel-bottomed streams; shallow areas of large lakes

Range: native to Europe from the Mediterranean to Arctic Norway and Siberia; widely introduced worldwide; Michigan—statewide

Food: insects, crayfish, small fish

Reproduction: It spawns October through December in stream headwaters and tributaries; stream mouths are used when migration is blocked; the female fans out saucer-shaped nest, the which male guards until spawning; the female covers the eggs.

Record and Average Size: Michigan State Record—41.5 lb., 43.75 in.; Average Size—2 to 6 lb., 10 to 20 in.

Fishing ⬭ Tip: A very small spinner tied just ahead of a black-and-gray streamer will sometimes wake up sluggish Brown Trout.

Notes: This European trout was brought to North America in 1883 and Michigan shortly after. A favorite of anglers, it is a secretive, hard-to-catch fish that fights hard and has a fine, delicate flavor. It often feeds aggressively on cloudy, rainy days and at night. It tolerates warmer, cloudier water than other trout, allowing it to live in the lower reaches of coldwater streams. Though it can survive in 80-degree water for a short time, it prefers the 50s to lower 60s. It hybridizes with Brook Trout to produce the sterile Tiger Trout. **91**

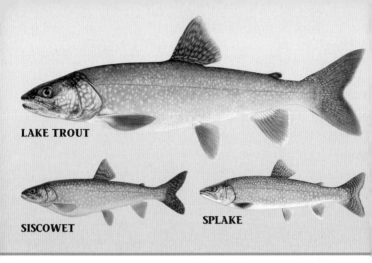

LAKE TROUT

SISCOWET

SPLAKE

Description: dark gray to gray-green on head, back, top fins, and tail; white spots on sides and unpaired fins; deeply forked tail; inside of mouth is white

Similar Species: Brook Trout (pg. 88), Splake, Siscowet

Lake Trout	Brook Trout	Lake Trout	Siscowet
sides lack worm-like markings	worm-like marks on back	body length greater than 4 times depth	body length less than 4 times depth

Lake Trout	Brook Trout	Splake
tail deeply forked	tail square to slightly forked	tail moderately forked

Salmonidae

LAKE TROUT
Salvelinus namaycush

Other Names: togue, mackinaw, great gray trout, laker

Habitat: cold (less than 65 degrees), oxygen-rich waters of deep, clear, infertile lakes

Range: the Great Lakes north through Canada and the northeastern US; stocked in some Rocky Mountain lakes; Michigan—Lakes Superior, Michigan, and a few northwestern Lower Peninsula lakes.

Food: small fish, insects

Reproduction: Females scatter eggs over rocky lake bottoms when the fall water temperatures get below 50 degrees.

Record and Average Size: Michigan state record—61.5 lb., 49 in.; Average Size—2 to 10 lb. and 15 to 20 in.

Fishing Tip: In early spring Lake Trout can be caught almost anywhere along Lake Superior shores by floating dead smelt just off the bottom.

Notes: This Michigan native is more closely related to char than trout. Lake Michigan once supported a large commercial Lake Trout fishery, but the species no longer reproduces naturally in the lake. The population was decimated in the mid-1950s by overfishing and the introduction of the Sea Lamprey. The Lake Michigan lake trout fishery is now maintained by a vigorous stocking program. A high-fat subspecies called the Siscowet or "fat" Lake Trout (*Salvelinus namaycush siscowet*) inhabits the deep waters of Lake Superior and may spend its life in water no warmer than 40 degrees.

93

Description: blue-green to brown head and back; silver lower sides, often with pink to rose stripe; sides, back, dorsal fins, and tail are covered with small black spots

Similar Species: Brown Trout (pg. 90), Brook Trout (pg. 88), Pink Salmon (pg. 100), Chinook Salmon (pg. 96)

Rainbow Trout	**Brown Trout**	**Rainbow Trout**	**Brook Trout**
pinkish stripe on silvery body	sides lack pinkish stripe	lacks worm-like markings	worm-like marks on back

Rainbow Trout	**Pink Salmon**	**Chinook Salmon**
white mouth	dark tongue and jaw tip	black or dark gray mouth

RAINBOW TROUT
Oncorhynchus mykiss

Salmonidae

Other Names: steelhead, Pacific trout, silver trout, 'bow

Habitat: prefers whitewater in cool streams and coastal regions of large lakes; tolerates smaller cool, clear lakes

Range: Pacific Ocean and coastal streams from Mexico to Alaska and northeast Russia; introduced worldwide; Michigan—statewide

Food: insects, small crustaceans, and fish

Reproduction: Predominantly a spring spawner, some fall-spawning varieties have been introduced into the state; females build nests in well-aerated gravel in both streams and lakes.

Record and Average Size: Michigan State Record—26.5 lb., 39.5 in.; Average Size—8 oz. to 6 lb., 10 to 20 in.

Fishing Tip: Small red spinners tipped with a minnow work well in inland lakes stocked with trout.

Notes: The Rainbow Trout was introduced from the Pacific Northwest and is now one of Michigan's most important sport fish. Rainbows reproduce naturally in Michigan, but much of the state's fishery is maintained by stocking. Rainbow Trout that spend their life in the open ocean or lakes, then migrate up streams to spawn are known as Steelheads. Kamloops (loopers) are a variety of Steelhead Trout used in stocking.

95

Description: iridescent green to blue-green back and upper sides, silver below lateral line; small spots on back and tail; inside of mouth is dark; breeding males are olive brown to purple with pronounced kype (hooked snout)

Similar Species: Coho Salmon (pg. 98), Pink Salmon (pg. 100), Rainbow Trout (pg. 94)

Chinook Salmon

small spots throughout tail

Coho Salmon

spots only in top half of tail

Pink Salmon

eye-size spots throughout tail

Chinook Salmon

inside of mouth is dark

Coho Salmon

inside of mouth is gray

Rainbow Trout

inside of mouth is white

CHINOOK SALMON
Oncorhynchus tshawytscha

Other Names: king, spring salmon, tyee, quinnat, black mouth

Habitat: open ocean; large, clear, gravel-bottomed rivers, and large lakes

Range: Pacific Ocean north from California to Japan; introduced to the Atlantic Coast in Maine and Great Lakes; Michigan—Lakes Superior and Michigan

Food: fish, some crustaceans

Reproduction: Chinooks in the Great Lakes mature in 3 to 5 years; in October and November they migrate up streams to attempt nesting on gravel bars; adults die shortly after.

Record and Average Size: Michigan State Record—46.06 lb., 43.5 in.; Average Size—8 to 15 lb., 24 to 30 in.

Fishing ⬭ Tip: Salmon seem to be picky about color; keep changing lure color when the bite is slow.

Notes: The largest member of the salmon family, Chinooks may reach 40 pounds in landlocked lakes. Prior to the 1960s many unsuccessful attempts were made to introduce Chinook salmon into the Great Lakes region. Since 1965, a stable population of hatchery-reared fish have been maintained in Lake Superior and Lake Michigan, creating the most important sport fishery in the state. Michigan Chinooks mature in four years and have fall spawning runs.

Description: dark metallic blue to green back; silver sides and belly; small dark spots on back, sides, and upper half of tail; inside of mouth is gray; breeding adults gray to green on head with red-maroon on sides, males develop kype (hooked snout)

Similar Species: Chinook Salmon (pg. 96), Pink Salmon (pg. 100), Rainbow Trout (pg. 94)

Coho Salmon

spots only in top half of tail

Chinook Salmon

small spots throughout tail

Pink Salmon

eye-size spots throughout tail

Coho Salmon

inside of mouth is gray

Rainbow Trout

inside of mouth is white

COHO SALMON
Oncorhynchus kisutch

Other Names: silver salmon, sea trout, blueback

Habitat: open ocean near clear, gravel-bottomed spawning streams; Great Lakes within 10 miles of shore

Range: Pacific Ocean north from California to Japan, Atlantic coast of US and Great Lakes; Michigan—Lake Superior, Lake Michigan and tributary streams during spawning

Food: smelt, alewives, and other fish

Reproduction: It spawns in October and November; adults migrate up tributary streams to build nests on gravel bars; parent fish die shortly after spawning.

Records and Average Size: Michigan State Record—30.56 lb, 40 in.; Average Size—3 to 5 lb., 14 to 20 in.

Fishing Tip: In spring, fishing gold spoons from breakwalls can be productive.

Notes: A very strong fighter and excellent table fare, the Coho was stocked in the Great Lakes by the Michigan DNR in 1965. There is little natural reproduction in Lake Superior steams due to the cold water temperatures and waterfalls that block migration to suitable spawning beds. In addition to stocking, natural reproduction in other areas of the Great Lakes helps support a popular fishery.

Description: steel-blue to blue-green back with silver sides; dark spots on back and tail, some as large as the eye; breeding males develop a large hump in front of the dorsal fin and a hooked upper jaw (kype); both sexes are pink during spawning

Similar Species: Chinook Salmon (pg. 96), Coho Salmon (pg. 98), Brown Trout (pg. 90), Rainbow Trout (pg. 94)

Pink Salmon **Chinook Salmon** **Coho Salmon**

| eye-size spots throughout tail | small spots throughout tail | spots only in top half of tail |

Pink Salmon **Coho Salmon** **Brown Trout** **Rainbow Trout**

dark tongue and jaw tip   inside of mouth is gray   inside of mouth is white   inside of mouth is white

PINK SALMON
Oncorhynchus gorbuscha

Other Names: humpback salmon, humpy, autumn salmon

Habitat: coastal Pacific Ocean and open water of the Great Lakes; spawns in clear streams

Range: coastal Pacific Ocean from northern California to Alaska; introduced to Great Lakes; Michigan—Lakes Superior and Michigan

Food: small fish, crustaceans

Reproduction: It spawns in fall in tributary streams, usually at two years of age; the female builds a nest on a gravel bar, then covers fertilized eggs; adults die after spawning.

Record and Average Size: Michigan State Record—8.56 lb., 28 in.; Average Size—1 to 2 lb., 14 to 18 in.

Fishing ⬤ Tip: Small, bright, active lures may entice non-feeding spawners to strike.

Notes: This Pacific salmon was unintentionally released into Thunder Bay in 1956 and has since spread throughout the Great Lakes. It spends two to three years in the open lake and then moves into streams to spawn and die. Often seen along the lakeshore during the odd-year spawning run; it is less common in even years. Pink Salmon are not often caught by anglers and are not considered great table fare; the flesh deteriorates rapidly and must be quickly put on ice.

101

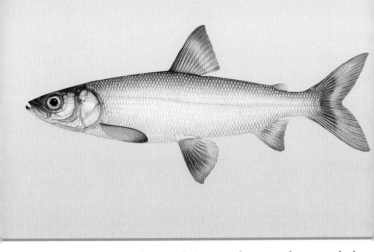

Description: sides silver with faint pink or purple tinge; dark back; light-colored tail; small mouth; long body but deeper than Rainbow Smelt

Similar Species: Lake Whitefish (pg. 104); Mooneye (pg. 70), Rainbow Smelt (pg. 110)

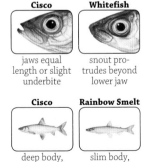

Cisco	**Lake Whitefish**	**Cisco**	**Mooneye**
jaws equal length or slight underbite	snout protrudes beyond lower jaw	adipose fin	lacks adipose fin

Cisco	**Rainbow Smelt**
deep body, inconspicuous teeth	slim body, prominent teeth

CISCO
Coregonus artedi

Other Names: shallow water, common or Great Lakes cisco; lake herring, tullibee

Habitat: shoal waters of the Great Lakes and nutrient-poor inland lakes with oxygen-rich depths that remain cool during the summer

Range: northeastern US, Great Lakes and Canada; Michigan—Lakes Superior, Michigan, and some deep inland lakes

Food: plankton, small crustaceans, aquatic insects

Reproduction: It spawns in November and December when water temperatures reach the lower 30s; eggs are deposited over clean bottoms, usually in 3 to 8 feet of water.

Record and Average Size: Michigan State Record—6.36 lb., 21.8 in.; Average Size—12 to 16 oz., 10 to 14 in.

Fishing ⬤ Tip: Tullibees respond well to tiny spinner baits when mayflies are emerging.

Notes: Ciscoes were once the most productive commercial fish in the Great Lakes. They are still common in Superior but threatened in Lake Michigan. Much of the "smoked whitefish" sold today is really cisco. The inland forms of ciscoes are known as tullibees and vary greatly in size and shape from one lake to another. Ciscoes can be caught through the ice in winter, or by fly-fishing in the summer.

Description: silver with dark brown to olive back and tail; snout protrudes past lower jaw; mouth is small, with two small flaps between the openings of each nostril

Similar Species: Cisco (pg. 102), Mooneye (pg. 70), Rainbow Smelt (pg. 110)

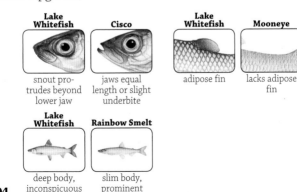

Lake Whitefish	Cisco		Lake Whitefish	Mooneye
snout protrudes beyond lower jaw	jaws equal length or slight underbite		adipose fin	lacks adipose fin

Lake Whitefish	Rainbow Smelt
deep body, inconspicuous teeth	slim body, prominent teeth

LAKE WHITEFISH
Coregonus clupeaformis

Salmonidae

Other Names: eastern, common, or Great Lakes whitefish; gizzard fish, Sault whitefish

Habitat: large, deep, clean inland lakes with cool, oxygen-rich depths during the summer; shallow areas of the Great Lakes

Range: from the Great Lakes north across North America; Michigan—Lake Superior, Lake Michigan, and a few large inland lakes in the northeast

Food: zooplankton, insects, small fish

Reproduction: It spawns on shallow gravel bars in late fall when water temperatures reach the low 30s; it occasionally ascends streams to spawn.

Record and Average Size: Michigan State Record—14.28 lbs., 31.75 in.; Average Size—2 to 5 lb., 10 to 18 in.

Fishing ⬤ Tip: When fishing inland lakes, whitefish can be caught by fishing small minnows in the deepest parts of the lake in late summer.

Notes: The largest whitefish in North America, the Lake Whitefish was historically the most important food fish in Michigan—first for the Native Americans (the most renowned fishery being at Sault St. Marie), then for early commercial fishermen. The whitefish population was greatly reduced by the 1950s, by debris from sawmills, which covered spawning beds, as well as by overfishing and the introduction of the Sea Lamprey.

105

Description: blotchy brown body; large mouth; eyes set almost on top of the broad head; large, wing-like pectoral fins; lacks scales

Similar Species: Round Goby (pg. 48)

Mottled Sculpin

lacks scales

Round Goby

scales on body

MOTTLED SCULPIN
Cottus bairdii

Cottidae

Other Names: common sculpin, muddler, or gudgeon

Habitat: cool, mineral-rich streams and clear lakes; favors areas with rocks and vegetation

Range: the eastern US through Canada to the Hudson Bay and the Rocky Mountains; Michigan—statewide

Food: aquatic invertebrates, fish eggs, small fish

Reproduction: It spawns in April and May in water that's 63 to 74 degrees; the male fans out a cavity beneath a rock, ledge, or log and attracts females via vigorous courtship displays; spawning fish turn upside down and deposit eggs on the underside of nest cover; the male guards and cleans the eggs after spawning.

Record and Average Size: Michigan State Record—none; Average Size—4 to 5 in.

Fishing Tip: Sculpins are good Lake Trout bait in the spring but are hard to collect.

Notes: Most of the 300 species of sculpins in North America are marine fish. There are a few freshwater species spread across the US and Canada. The Mottled Sculpin is the most common sculpin in Michigan, but there are three other species: Spoonhead, Deepwater, and Slimy. Frequently found in trout streams, Sculpins were once thought to prey heavily on trout eggs, but several studies have shown this not to be true. The Deepwater Sculpin resides in the deeper portions of the Great Lakes and is an important food source for Lake Trout.

Description: long, thin body; sides bright silver with conspicuous black stripe; upturned mouth; two dorsal fins

Similar Species: Common Shiner (pg. 68), Rainbow Smelt (pg. 110)

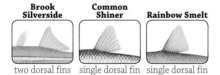

Brook Silverside   **Common Shiner**   **Rainbow Smelt**

two dorsal fins   single dorsal fin   single dorsal fin

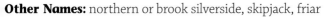

BROOK SILVERSIDE
Labidesthes sicculus

Atherinopsidae

Other Names: northern or brook silverside, skipjack, friar

Habitat: surface of clear lakes and large streams

Range: southeastern US to the Great Lakes; Michigan—the southern third of state

Food: aquatic and flying insects, spiders

Reproduction: It spawns in late spring and early summer; eggs are laid in sticky strings that attach to vegetation; adults die soon after spawning.

Record and Average Size: Michigan State Record—none; Average Size—2 to 4 in.

Fishing Tip: Silversides are not good as bait. They are not hardy and tend to jump out of the bait pail.

Notes: The Brook Silverside belongs to a large family of fish that is mostly tropical or subtropical, with many species found in saltwater. It is a flashy fish often seen cruising near the surface in small schools. Its upturned mouth is an adaptation for surface feeding. It is not uncommon to see a Brook Silverside leap from the water in pursuit of prey, flying-fish style.

Description: large mouth with prominent teeth; jaw extends to rear margin of the eye; dark green back; violet-blue sides and white belly; deeply forked tail; adipose fin

Similar Species: Cisco (pg. 102), Lake Whitefish (pg. 104), Common Shiner (pg. 68), Brook Silverside (pg. 108)

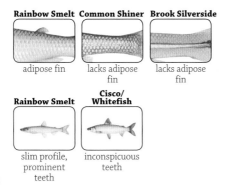

Rainbow Smelt	Common Shiner	Brook Silverside
adipose fin	lacks adipose fin	lacks adipose fin

Rainbow Smelt	Cisco/ Whitefish
slim profile, prominent teeth	inconspicuous teeth

RAINBOW SMELT
Osmerus mordax

Other Names: ice or frost fish, lake herring, leefish

Habitat: open oceans and large lakes; tributaries at spawning

Range: coastal Pacific, Atlantic, and Arctic Oceans; land-locked in northeastern US and southeastern Canada; Michigan—the Great Lakes and a few large inland lakes

Food: crustaceans, insect larvae, small fish

Reproduction: Spawning takes place in May, at night, in the first mile of tributary streams.

Record and Average Size: Michigan State Record—none; Average Size—5 to 10 in.

Fishing ⬭ Tip: Smelt are good Lake Trout bait; fish them near the bottom in early spring.

Notes: Smelt are saltwater fish that enter freshwater to spawn. In 1912 they were successfully introduced into Howe, Crystal, and Trout Lakes to support the introduced salmon stock. Smelt soon escaped into Lake Michigan and were found in Green Bay in 1924. This small fish was soon making spectacular spawning runs and smelt fishing became a spring ritual. The Great Lakes smelt population crashed in the 1980s and has not fully recovered.

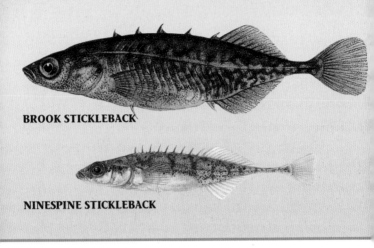

BROOK STICKLEBACK

NINESPINE STICKLEBACK

Description: both Brook and Ninespine Sticklebacks are brown with torpedo-shaped bodies and a very narrow caudal peduncle (the area just before the tail); the front portion of dorsal fin has short, separated spines; pelvic fins are abdominal and reduced to a single spine; small, sharp teeth

Similar Species: Brook Stickleback, Ninespine Stickleback

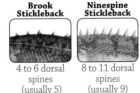

Brook Stickleback	Ninespine Stickleback
4 to 6 dorsal spines (usually 5)	8 to 11 dorsal spines (usually 9)

STICKLEBACKS

Culaea inconstans, Pungitius pungitius

Gasterosteidae

Other Names: common stickleback, spiny minnow

Habitat: shallows of cool streams and lakes

Range: Kansas through the northern US and Canada; Michigan—statewide

Food: small aquatic animals, occasionally algae

Reproduction: When water reaches 50 to 68 degrees, the male builds a golf-ball-size, globular nest of sticks, algae, and other plant matter on submerged vegetation; females deposit eggs and depart, often plowing a hole in the side of the nest in the process; the male repairs any damage and viciously guards the eggs until hatching; an ambitious male may build a second, larger nest and transfer the eggs.

Record and Average Size: Michigan State Record—none; Average Size—1 to 3 in.

Fishing Tip: Sticklebacks are often found mixed in with crappie minnows and are discarded by anglers, but they are fine as bait.

Notes: Most members of the stickleback family are marine fish, but some are equally at home in fresh or saltwater. The Brook Stickleback is Michigan's most common stickleback and can be found in most streams and lakes in the state. The Ninespine Stickleback is found in the Great Lakes and are increasing in numbers in Lake Michigan. These pugnacious little predators will readily build and defend nests in captivity but should not be taken from the wild.

Description: slate gray to brown sides, white belly; bony plates on skin; tail lacks plates and is shark-like with upper lobe longer than lower; blunt snout with four barbels; spiracles (openings between eye and corner of gill)

Similar Species: Shovelnose Sturgeon

Lake Sturgeon

Shovelnose Sturgeon

spiracle between eye and gill

lacks spiracles

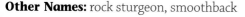

LAKE STURGEON
Acipenser fulvescens

Other Names: rock sturgeon, smoothback

Habitat: quiet waters of large rivers and lakes

Range: Hudson Bay, the Great Lakes, the Mississippi and Missouri River drainages southeast to Alabama; Michigan—Lakes Superior, Michigan, Huron, and a few large tributary streams

Food: snails, clams, crayfish, aquatic insects

Reproduction: It spawns in April through June in lake shallows and tributary streams; a single female may produce up to 1 million eggs.

Record and Average Size: Michigan State Record—193 lb., 87 in.; Average Size—10 to 30 lb., 20 to 40 in.

Fishing ⬭ Tip: Large grayfish tails are good sturgeon bait.

Notes: The Lake Sturgeon is the largest fish found in Michigan, and it has historically reached weights of more than 200 pounds. Today, due to commercial fishing, dams, habitat alteration, and pollution, this slow-growing fish only averages 5 to 40 pounds. Sturgeon are primitive fish that have cartilage in place of bones, and bony plates in place of scales. These slow-growing fish don't reproduce until they are 20 years old and may live to be 75 or older.

Description: olive-brown to bronze back; sides dull olive fading to white belly; blunt snout; rounded head; long dorsal fin; upper lip even with lower margin of eye

Similar Species: Common Carp (pg. 60), Black Buffalo (pg. 118), Smallmouth Buffalo

Bigmouth Buffalo

upper lip level with lower edge of eye

Black Buffalo

upper lip well below eye

Smallmouth Buffalo

upper lip well below eye

Bigmouth Buffalo

forward-facing mouth, lacks barbels

Common Carp

downturned mouth with barbels

BIGMOUTH BUFFALO

Ictiobus cyprinellus

Other Names: baldpate, blue router, round buffalo

Habitat: soft-bottomed shallows of large lakes, sloughs, and oxbows; slow-flowing streams and rivers

Range: Saskatchewan to Lake Erie south through the Mississippi River drainage to the Gulf of Mexico; Michigan—Lake Erie and a few streams in southeast corner of state

Food: small mollusks, insect larvae, zooplankton

Reproduction: It makes spectacular spawning runs in clear, shallow water of flooded fields and marshes during April and May; spawns when water temperatures reach the low 60s.

Record and Average Size: Michigan State Record—33 lb., 35.25 in.; Average Size—10 to 15 lb., 18 to 24 in.

Fishing ⬤ Tip: Buffalo are filter feeders that are hard to hook but can be caught by floating small pieces of nightcrawlers in slow-moving backwaters.

Notes: The Bigmouth Buffalo is a schooling, big-water fish that inhabits large, shallow lakes and streams. Historically the presence of Bigmouth Buffalo in Michigan is unclear, but they were stocked in some of the lower Great Lakes in the early 1900s and are commercially fished in Lake Erie. The presence of Smallmouth Buffalo in Michigan is also unclear, but there may be some or hybrids in Lake Michigan. These large Michigan suckers can withstand low oxygen levels, high water temperatures, and some turbidity, but they prefer cool, clean water for foraging.

Description: slate green to dark gray back; sides have a blue-bronze sheen; deep body with a sloping back that supports a long dorsal fin; upper lip well below eye

Similar Species: Common Carp (pg. 60), Smallmouth Buffalo

Black Buffalo

upper lip well below eye

Bigmouth Buffalo

upper lip level with lower edge of eye

Smallmouth Buffalo

upper lip well below eye

Black Buffalo

mouth lacks barbels

Common Carp

barbels below mouth

118

BLACK BUFFALO
Ictiobus niger

Other Names: buoy tender; current or deep-water buffalo

Habitat: deep, fast water of large streams; deep sloughs, backwaters, and impoundments

Range: the lower Great Lakes and the Mississippi River drainage west to South Dakota, south to New Mexico and Louisiana; Michigan—Lake Michigan, Lake Huron, Lake Erie, and streams in southern half of state

Food: aquatic insects, crustaceans, algae

Reproduction: Spawning takes place in April and May; fish move up tributaries to lay eggs in flooded sloughs and marshes.

Record and Average Size: Michigan State Record—46.54 lb., 38.5 in.; Average Size—8 to 10 lb., 15 to 24 in.

Fishing ⬤ Tip: Fish the mouth of tributary streams with small baits during the spawning run.

Notes: Black Buffalo are rare to uncommon in Michigan; the Michigan population is separate from the main population, which is located in the Mississippi River drainage. Black Buffalo are one of the largest naturally occurring fish in Michigan. They inhabit the deep, strong currents of large rivers (hence the nickname Current Buffalo). It is rarely caught on hook and line, but it's notable because of its size and strong fight. Black Buffalo can hybridize with Smallmouth Buffalo.

Description: bright silver, often with a yellow tinge; fins clear; deep body with a round, blunt head; leading rays of dorsal fin extend into a large, arching "quill"

Similar Species: Common Carp (pg. 60), Smallmouth Buffalo

Quillback

mouth lacks
barbels

Common Carp

barbels below
mouth

Quillback

longest dorsal
ray similar to
length of base

Smallmouth Buffalo

longest dorsal
ray much
shorter than
base

QUILLBACK
Carpiodes cyprinus

Other Names: silver carp, carpsucker, lake quillback

Habitat: slow-flowing streams and rivers; backwaters and lakes, particularly areas with soft bottoms

Range: south-central Canada through the Great Lakes to the eastern US, south through the Mississippi River drainage to the Gulf; Michigan—Lake Michigan, Lake Huron, and Lake Erie and drainage streams in the Lower Peninsula

Food: insects, plant matter, decaying material on bottom

Reproduction: It ascends tributaries from late spring through early summer; it spawns over sand, gravel, or mud.

Record and Average Size: Michigan State Record—9.15 lb., 24.75 in.; Average Size—1 to 3 lb., 10 to 15 in.

Fishing ⬤ Tip: In clear streams, drift small pieces of night-crawlers into the pools below riffles.

Notes: There are four species of carpsuckers in North America; the Quillback is the only one that resides in Michigan. Quillbacks are common in many soft-bottomed streams and lakes in Michigan, and though reportedly of good flavor are not of much interest to anglers. This pretty silver fish travels in schools and feeds by filtering through bottom debris.

Description: olive-brown to brownish back; sides silver to bronze; white belly; bright red tail; blunt nose; sickle-shaped dorsal fin

Similar Species: Longnose Sucker (pg. 124), White Sucker (pg. 126)

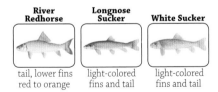

River Redhorse	Longnose Sucker	White Sucker
tail, lower fins red to orange	light-colored fins and tail	light-colored fins and tail

RIVER REDHORSE

Moxostoma carinatum

Other Names: redhorse, redfin sucker

Habitat: clean streams and rivers with sand, gravel, or rocky bottom; occasionally in clear lakes

Range: the Great Lakes states to New England south to the Gulf; Michigan—statewide

Food: insects, crustaceans, mussels, plant debris

Reproduction: It spawns from late May to June in small tributary streams; the male builds a 4- to 8-foot-diameter nest on gravel shoals, then courts females by darting back and forth across the nest; a second male may join the display and spawning process.

Record and Average Size: Michigan State Record—12.89 lb., 29.25 in.; Average Size—2 to 6 lb., 12 to 18 in.

Fishing ⬭ Tip: Fish wet flies or worms in rocky, fast water.

Notes: The River Redhorse is the most common of the six redhorse species found in Michigan. It can be distinguished from the others by its bright-red tail. All are "sucker-type fish" that are rather similar in appearance. They may all look alike, but each is a separate species and occupies its own niche in Michigan waters. All the redhorses are clean-water fish and very susceptible to increased turbidity and pollutants. They all fight well on light tackle and are good when smoked.

Description: black, brown to dark olive back; slate to pale
   brown sides fading to white belly; males develop a red band
   during breeding; long snout protruding beyond upper lip

Similar Species: River Redhorse (pg. 122), White Sucker
   (pg. 126)

Longnose Sucker
snout extends well beyond upper lip

White Sucker
snout barely extends past upper lip

Longnose Sucker
fins white to yellowish

River Redhorse
fins red to orange

LONGNOSE SUCKER
Catostomus catostomus

Other Names: sturgeon, red, or redside sucker

Habitat: primarily shallow waters of large, cold lakes and streams, occasionally in deep water

Range: Siberia across Canada through Great Lakes to the eastern US; Missouri and Columbia River systems in the West; Michigan—Lake Superior, Michigan, Huron, and tributary streams

Food: small crustaceans, plant material

Reproduction: It spawns in April and May, when fish crowd small tributary streams.

Record and Average Size: Michigan State Record—6.88 lb., 22.5 in.; Average Size—1 to 2 lb., 10 to 16 in.

Fishing ⬤ Tip: Drift yellow Trout PowerBait among the rocks in river eddies.

Notes: Longnose Suckers are northern cold-water fish found in both North America and Northern Europe. Though primarily known as a shallow-water fish, it has been taken as deep as 600 feet in Lake Superior. Large numbers of Longnose Suckers crowd some streams during the spawning run. The Longnose Sucker is delicious smoked, and smoked fish connoisseurs argue that it is superior to the White Sucker in flavor.

Description: back olive to brown; sides gray to silver; belly white; gray dorsal fin and tail; other fins clear or whitish; rounded head; blunt snout

Similar Species: Longnose Sucker (pg. 124), River Redhorse (pg. 122)

White Sucker

snout barely extends past upper lip

Longnose Sucker

snout extends well beyond upper lip

White Sucker

light-colored lower fins

River Redhorse

fins red to orange

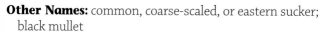

WHITE SUCKER
Catostomus commersonii

Other Names: common, coarse-scaled, or eastern sucker; black mullet

Habitat: clean lakes and streams with some rock or gravel areas for spawning

Range: Canada through central and eastern US south to a line from New Mexico to South Carolina; Michigan—statewide

Food: insects, crustaceans, plant matter

Reproduction: It spawns over gravel or coarse sand in April and early May; adults migrate up small tributaries; in large lakes spawning may occur along shoreline shallows.

Record and Average Size: Michigan State Record—7.19 lb., 28 in.; Average Size—1 to 3 lb., 12 to 18 in.

Fishing Tip: In early spring, fish the mouth of small streams with worms.

Notes: The White Sucker is one of the most common fish in Michigan. It is commercially harvested for both animal and human consumption, and it is also a mainstay in the bait industry. White Suckers are not the great consumers of trout eggs they were once thought to be. When first hatched, White Suckers may compete with trout fry for food, but their tremendous value as a food source for game fish offsets this competition.

Description: dark green back, greenish sides often with dark lateral band; belly white to gray; large, forward-facing mouth; lower jaw extends to rear margin of eye

Similar Species: Smallmouth Bass (pg. 130)

Largemouth Bass	Smallmouth Bass
mouth extends beyond dark orange eye	mouth does not extend beyond red eye

LARGEMOUTH BASS

Micropterus salmoides

Other Names: black bass, green bass, green trout, slough bass

Habitat: shallow, fertile, weedy lakes and river backwaters

Range: southern Canada through US into Mexico; widely introduced worldwide; Michigan—statewide

Food: small fish, frogs, crayfish, insects, leeches

Reproduction: In May and June when water temperatures reach 60 degrees, the male builds a nest in 2 to 8 feet of water, usually on firm bottom in weedy cover; the male guards the eggs and fry until the "brood swarm" disperses.

Record and Average Size: Michigan State Record: 11.94 lb., 27 in.; Average Size—1 to 3 lb., 10 to 20 in.

Fishing ⬤ Tip: For large bass, fish at night with large noisy surface plugs.

Notes: The most popular game fish in the United States, the Largemouth Bass is a voracious predator, found in lakes and streams throughout Michigan. A denizen of the weeds, it will eat anything that will fit in its mouth. Bass are strong fighters and often jump from the water when hooked. Largemouths are not noted for table quality when large, but are delicious when under 2 pounds and taken from clear water.

Description: back and sides mottled dark green to bronze or pale gold, often with dark vertical bands; white belly; stout body; large, forward-facing mouth; red eye

Similar Species: Largemouth Bass (pg. 128)

	Smallmouth Bass	**Largemouth Bass**

mouth does not extend beyond red eye

mouth extends beyond dark orange eye

SMALLMOUTH BASS

Micropterus dolomieu

Centrarchidae

Other Names: bronzeback, brown or redeye bass, redeye, white or mountain trout

Habitat: clear, swift-flowing streams and rivers; clear lakes with gravel or rocky shorelines

Range: extensively introduced throughout the world; Michigan—statewide

Food: small fish, crayfish, insects, frogs

Reproduction: In May and June, when water temperature reaches mid- to high 60s, the male sweeps out a nest in a gravel bed, typically in 3 to 10 feet of water; the nest is often next to a log or boulder; the male guards the nest and young until fry disperse.

Records and Average Size: Michigan State Record—9.98 lb., 23.1 in.; Average Size—1 to 3 lb., 10 to 20 in.

Fishing Tip: Fish crayfish imitation lures in the shade of large rocks or brush.

Notes: Smallmouth Bass are world-class game fish noted for strong fights and acrobatic jumps. Both Large and Smallmouth Bass have been widely introduced and are now important game fish throughout the world. It is best known as a fast-water stream fish, but there are good populations in clean lakes, including the shallows of the Great Lakes. Though the range of this slow-maturing fish has expanded, its numbers are decreasing in many areas due to overfishing and habitat loss.

131

Description: black to dark-olive back; silver sides with dark green or black blotches; its back is more arched and the depression above the eye is more pronounced than in the White Crappie

Similar Species: White Crappie (pg. 134)

Black Crappie
usually 7 to 8 spines in dorsal fin

White Crappie
usually 5 to 6 spines in dorsal fin

Black Crappie
dorsal fin length equal to distance from eye to dorsal

White Crappie
dorsal fin shorter than distance from eye to dorsal

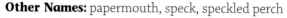

BLACK CRAPPIE

Pomoxis nigromaculatus

Centrarchidae

Other Names: papermouth, speck, speckled perch

Habitat: quiet, clear water of streams and mid-size lakes; often associated with vegetation but also roams deep, open basins and flats, particularly during winter

Range: southern Manitoba through the Atlantic and southeastern states; introduced in the West; Michigan—statewide

Food: small fish, aquatic insects, zooplankton

Reproduction: It spawns in shallow weed beds from May to June when water temperatures reach the high 50s; the male sweeps out a circular nest, typically on fine gravel or sand; the male guards the nest and fry; they may spawn in colonies.

Record and Average Size: Michigan State Record—4.12 lb.; Average Size—6 to 16 oz., 8 to 10 in.

Fishing Tip: Try very small jigs or wet flies when the bite is slow.

Notes: Pursued year-round by Michigan anglers for its sweet-tasting white fillets, it is an aggressive carnivore that will hit everything from waxworms and minnows to jigging spoons and small crankbaits. The Black Crappie actively feeds at night and often suspends well off the bottom in pursuit of plankton and baitfish. It requires clearer water and more vegetation than White Crappie.

133

Description: greenish back; silvery green to white sides with 7 to 9 dark vertical bars; the only sunfish with 6 spines in both the dorsal and anal fin

Similar Species: Black Crappie (pg. 132)

White Crappie	Black Crappie
usually 5 to 6 spines in dorsal fin	usually 7 to 8 spines in dorsal fin

White Crappie	Black Crappie
dorsal fin shorter than distance from eye to dorsal	dorsal fin length equal to distance from eye to dorsal

WHITE CRAPPIE

Pomoxis annularis

Centrarchidae

Other Names: silver, pale, or ringed crappie; papermouth

Habitat: slightly silty streams and midsize to large lakes; prefers less vegetation than the Black Crappie

Range: North Dakota south and east to the Gulf and Atlantic states except peninsular Florida; Michigan— the lower peninsula

Food: aquatic insects, small fish, plankton

Reproduction: It spawns on firm sand or gravel when the water temperature approaches 60 degrees; the male builds a shallow, round nest and guards eggs and young after spawning.

Record and Average Size: Michigan State Record—3.39 lb., 19.5 in.; Average Size—5 to 14 oz., 6 to 9 in.

Fishing ⬭ Tip: In midsummer, slowly troll minnows far behind the boat to locate schools.

Notes: White Crappies are the southern cousin of Black Crappies, preferring deeper, less weedy water and can tolerate more turbidity. They have been introduced into a few lakes in the U.P. but are not very successful there. Both Black and White Crappies actively feed during the winter, ensuring that they are two of the most popular panfish during the ice fishing season.

Description: dark olive to green on back, blending to silver-gray, copper, orange, purple or brown on sides; 5 to 9 dark vertical bars on sides that fade with age; yellow belly and copper breast; large dark gill spot that extends completely to gill margin; dark spot on rear margin of dorsal fin

Similar Species: Green Sunfish (pg. 138), Pumpkinseed (pg. 144)

Bluegill

small mouth

Green Sunfish

large mouth

Bluegill

dark gill spot

Pumpkinseed

orange crescent

Bluegill

dark spot on dorsal fin

Pumpkinseed

no dark spot

136

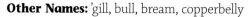

BLUEGILL

Lepomis macrochirus

Other Names: 'gill, bull, bream, copperbelly

Habitat: medium to large streams and most lakes with weedy bays or shorelines

Range: southern Canada into Mexico; Michigan—statewide

Food: insects, small fish, leeches, snails, zooplankton, algae

Reproduction: It spawns from late May to early August; the male excavates a nest in gravel or coarse sand, often in shallow weeds, in colonies of up to 50 nests; often, a smaller "cuckholder" male darts into the nest and fertilizes eggs; the male guards the nest until fry disperse.

Records and Average Size: Michigan State Record—2.75 lb., 13.75 in; Average Size—5 to 10 oz., 6 to 10 in.

Fishing Tip: Adding a kernel of corn to your bait will sometimes entice large Bluegills in schools of small ones.

Notes: Bluegills are one of the most popular panfish in Michigan and throughout the United States. Small fish are easy to catch near docks in summer, but larger "bulls" favor deep weed beds close to open water. Bluegills frequently hybridize with other sunfish. All sunfish have acute daytime vision for feeding on small prey items but see poorly in low light.

137

Description: dark green back; dark-olive to bluish sides; yellow to cream belly; scales flecked with yellow, producing a brassy appearance; dark gill spot with pale margin; large mouth with thick lips

Similar Species: Bluegill (pg. 136)

Green Sunfish

large mouth

Bluegill

small mouth

GREEN SUNFISH
Lepomis cyanellus

Other Names: green perch, blue-spotted sunfish, sand bass

Habitat: warm, weedy shallow lakes and the backwaters of slow-moving streams

Range: most of the US into Mexico, excluding Florida and the Rocky Mountains; Michigan—statewide

Food: aquatic insects, crustaceans, small fish

Reproduction: Beginning in May and June, the male fans out a nest on gravel bottom, often in less than 1 foot of water, near weeds or other cover; the male may grunt to lure a female into the nest; after spawning, the male guards the nest and fry.

Record and Average Size: Michigan State Record—1.53 lb., 10 in.; Average Size—4 to 10 oz., 3 to 7 in.

Fishing ⬤ Tip: At times, green or yellow trout PowerBait is good for sunfish.

Notes: Green Sunfish are often mistaken for Bluegills but prefer shallower weed beds. They are very common in southern Michigan lakes, though they are completely absent from some water bodies. Green Sunfish stunt easily, filling some lakes with 3-inch-long "potato chips." Green Sunfish hybridize with Bluegills and Pumpkinseeds, producing large, aggressive offspring.

Description: dark-greenish blue back; light green sides flecked with green and yellow; belly and chest bright orange to pale yellow; gill flap tapers to long black finger

Similar Species: Redear Sunfish (pg. 146)

Longear Sunfish	**Redear Sunfish**	**Longear Sunfish**	**Redear Sunfish**
dark spots on dorsal fin	no spots on dorsal fin	blue-green bands on side of head	solid green to bronze head

LONGEAR SUNFISH

Lepomis megalotis

Other Names: Great Lakes Longear, blue-and-orange sunfish, red perch

Habitat: clear, moderately weedy, slow-moving shallow streams and clear lakes

Range: central US north to Quebec, then east to the Appalachian Mountains and as far south as the Gulf of Mexico; introduced into some western states; Michigan—Lower Peninsula

Food: small insects, crustaceans and fish

Reproduction: Males build and guard nests on shallow gravel beds when water temperatures reach the mid-70s.

Record and Average Size: Michigan state record—none; Average Size—5 oz., 3 to 4 in.

Fishing ⬤ Tip: Easy to catch with any very small bait.

Notes: A colorful but secretive little sunfish, it prefers clear, slow-moving shallow streams, but it does inhabit clean lakes. A southern species, it reaches the limits of its range in the southern Great Lakes region. Longear Sunfish are disappearing from many streams due to increased siltation from agriculture. They feed on the surface more than other sunfish. There is some hybridization between Longears and other sunfish.

Description: bluish green back fading to orange; about 30 orange or red spots on sides of males, brown spots on females; orange pelvic and anal fins; black gill spot has light margin

Similar Species: Bluegill (pg. 136), Green Sunfish (pg. 138), Redear Sunfish (pg. 146)

Orangespotted Sunfish

light margin on gill spot

Bluegill

gill spot lacks light margin

Redear Sunfish

orange or red crescent on gill

Orangespotted Sunfish

hard spines longer than soft rays

Green Sunfish

hard spines shorter than soft rays

ORANGESPOTTED SUNFISH

Centrarchidae

Lepomis humilis

Other Names: orangespot, dwarf sunfish, pygmy sunfish

Habitat: open to moderately weedy pools in lakes and streams, prefers soft bottoms

Range: Southern Great Lakes through Mississippi River basin to Gulf states; Michigan—a few lakes and streams near Lake Erie

Food: insects, small crustaceans

Reproduction: The male builds and guards a nest in shallow water when water temperatures reach the mid-60s; they are colonial nesters.

Record and Average Size: Michigan State Record—none; Average Size—3 to 4 oz., 3 to 4 in.

Fishing Tip: These sunfish will bite almost anything, even small shiny bare hooks.

Notes: This brightly colored sunfish is very common in some lakes and although it is often caught, it is too small to be a significant panfish. The Orangespotted Sunfish is important as a forage species for other game fish and may be important for mosquito larvae control in some areas. It survives well in silty water and tolerates slight pollution, making it well suited for small lakes in agricultural areas.

Description: back brown to olive; sides speckled with orange, yellow, blue, and green spots with 7 to 10 vertical bands; chest and belly yellow or orange; black gill spot has light margin with orange or red crescent

Similar Species: Bluegill (pg. 136), Green Sunfish (pg. 138), Orangespotted Sunfish (pg. 142)

Pumpkinseed

orange or red crescent on gill flap

Bluegill

gill spot lacks light margin

Orangespotted Sunfish

light margin on gill spot

Pumpkinseed

long, pointed pectoral fin

Green Sunfish

rounded pectoral fin

144

PUMPKINSEED
Lepomis gibbosus

Other Names: 'seed, punky, yellow or round sunfish, bream

Habitat: weedy ponds, clear lakes, slow-moving streams; prefers slightly cooler water than Bluegill

Range: native to eastern and central North America, widely introduced elsewhere; Michigan—statewide

Food: insects, snails, fish, leeches, small amounts of vegetation

Reproduction: When water temperatures reach 55 to 63 degrees the male builds a nest in gravel among weeds in less than 2 feet of water; nests are located in colonies, often with other sunfish species; the male aggressively guards the nest; multiple broods per year are common.

Record and Average Size: Michigan State Record—2.15 lb., 12.6 in.; Average Size—6 to 10 oz., 5 to 10 in.

Fishing ⬤ Tip: Wax worms are good Pumpkinseed bait in both summer and winter.

Notes: The Pumpkinseed is one of the most beautiful fish in Michigan. It often schools under submerged logs or deadfalls and around docks. It is easy to catch on small natural and artificial baits, and it makes fine table fare. Larger specimens often feed along edges of deep weed beds during the day and settle to the bottom at night. Hybridization with other sunfish and stunting is common.

Description: back and sides bronze to dark green, fading to light green; faint vertical bars; bluish stripes on side of head; gill flap short with dark spot and red margin in males

Similar Species: Longear Sunfish (pg. 140), Bluegill (pg. 136)

Redear Sunfish

orange crescent on gill flap spot

Bluegill

dark margin on gill flap spot

Longear Sunfish

long dark gill flap

Redear Sunfish

no spots on dorsal fin

Longear Sunfish

dark spots on dorsal fin

REDEAR SUNFISH
Lepomis microlophus

Other Names: shellcracker, stumpknocker, yellow bream

Habitat: congregates around stumps and logs in low to sparse vegetation; redears prefer large, quiet lakes but are often introduced into farm ponds

Range: northern Midwest through southern US; introduced into some northern and western states; Michigan—the southern third of Lower Peninsula

Food: mainly mollusks

Reproduction: Males build and guard nests in shallow water in May and June, but they may reproduce well into the summer.

Record and Average Size: Michigan State Record—2.36 lb., 12.6 in.; Average Size—8 to 12 oz., 8 to 10 in.

Fishing Tip: Fish close to plant stalks and submerged tree branches.

Notes: The Redear Sunfish is a large, highly regarded southern panfish that was first introduced into Michigan in the 1950s. More were stocked in the 1980s, and a management plan was created in 1991. The introductions have been very successful, with Redears becoming the dominant panfish in some southern Michigan lakes.

Description: brown to olive-green back and sides with dark spots and overall bronze appearance; red eye; thicker, heavier body than other sunfish; large mouth

Similar Species: Bluegill (pg. 136), Green Sunfish (pg. 138), Pumpkinseed (pg. 144), Warmouth (pg. 150)

Rock Bass	**Green Sunfish**	**Pumpkinseed**	**Warmouth**
solid dark gill spot	light margin on gill spot	orange or red crescent on gill flap	dark gill spot with light margin

Rock Bass	**Bluegill**
large mouth extends to eye	small mouth does not extend to eye

ROCK BASS
Ambloplites rupestris

Other Names: redeye, goggle eye, rock sunfish

Habitat: vegetation on firm to rocky bottom in clear water lakes and medium-size streams

Range: southern Canada through central and eastern US to the northern edge of Gulf states; Michigan—statewide

Food: prefers crayfish, but eats aquatic insects and small fish

Reproduction: When water temperatures reach the high 60s to 70s, the male fans out a coarse gravel nest in weeds less than 3 feet deep; the male guards eggs and fry.

Record and Average Size: Michigan State Record—3.62 lb., 20 in.; Average Size—8 to 16 oz., 6 to 10 in.

Fishing Tip: Fish small dark green or brown-haired jigs on the bottom near weedy rock piles.

Notes: Rock Bass are common in Michigan's clear northern lakes but less common in the south. They prefer weed beds associated with rocks. Though the Rock Bass is plentiful, hard-fighting, and good tasting, it is seldom targeted by anglers. The flavor is a little stronger than Bluegill, but it is a willing biter and fun to catch on light tackle. The Rock Bass is often found in schools that do not stray far from their home territories.

149

Description: back and sides greenish gray to brown; lightly mottled with faint vertical bands; stout body; large mouth; red eye; 3 to 5 reddish-brown streaks radiate from eye

Similar Species: Bluegill (pg. 136), Green Sunfish (pg. 138), Pumpkinseed (pg. 144), Rock Bass (pg. 148)

Warmouth	**Bluegill**	**Green Sunfish**
jaw extends at least to middle of eye	small mouth does not extend to eye	jaw does not extend to middle of eye

Warmouth	**Pumpkinseed**	**Rock Bass**
light margin on gill spot	prominent orange or red crescent on gill spot	dark gill spot lacks light margin

WARMOUTH
Lepomis gulosus

Other Names: goggle-eye, wide-mouth sunfish, stump-knocker, weed bass

Habitat: heavy weeds in turbid lakes, reservoirs, and slow-moving streams

Range: southern US from Texas to Florida north to the southern Great Lakes region; Michigan—Great Lake drainages in southern Lower Peninsula

Food: small fish, insects, snails, crustaceans

Reproduction: The male fans out a solitary nest in dense, shallow weeds when water temperatures reach the low 70s; the nest is often located by a rock, stump, or weed clump; the male guards the eggs after spawning.

Record and Average Size: Michigan State Record—1.38 lb., 11 in.; Average Size—8 to 12 oz., 5 to 8 in.

Fishing ⬤ Tip: Fish with small jigs and keep them moving around stumps and logs.

Notes: The Warmouth is a southern panfish that reaches its northern limit in mid-Michigan. More tolerant of turbid water than other Michigan sunfish, they can withstand low oxygen levels, high silt loads, and water temperatures well into the 90s. Warmouths inhabit warm, shallow lakes and slow-moving streams. They are solitary fish that prefer dense weed beds to open water.

Description: dark gray back; bright silver sides with 7 or 8 indistinct or broken stripes; dorsal fin separated, front part of the dorsal has hard spines; the rear part has soft spines; two tooth patches on back of tongue

Similar Species: White Bass (pg. 154), Yellow Bass

White Bass Hybrid

two tooth patches, one on back of tongue

White Bass

lower jaw protrudes beyond snout

Yellow Bass

lower jaw even with snout

White Bass Hybrid

stripes indistinct or broken

White Bass

stripes continuous

Yellow Bass

stripes broken above anal fin

WHITE BASS HYBRID

Morone saxatilis X Morone chrysops

Moronidae

Other Names: white striper, wiper

Habitat: stocked in large rivers, lakes, and impoundments

Range: stocked in at least 40 states; Michigan—Lake Michigan and a few tributary streams in Lower Peninsula

Food: small fish

Reproduction: This hatchery-produced hybrid is not fertile.

Record and Average Size: Michigan state record—10.75 lb., 27.5 in.; Average size—2 to 6 lb., 12 to 18 in.

Fishing ⬤ Tip: Troll deep running silver lures to locate schools of fish.

Notes: The White Bass Hybrid is a hatchery raised fish; it is commonly a cross between a female Striped Bass and a male White Bass. They are not fertile and only occasionally will interbreed with the parent White Bass stock. This Hybrid is becoming an important aquaculture fish, supplying fillets for grocery stores and restaurants.

Description: bright silver; 6 to 8 distinct, uninterrupted black stripes on each side; front part of the dorsal fin has hard spines; the rear section is soft-rayed; lower jaw protrudes beyond snout

Similar Species: White Bass Hybrid (pg. 152), Yellow Bass

White Bass	White Bass Hybrid	Yellow Bass
lower jaw protrudes beyond snout	two tooth patches, one on back of tongue	lower jaw even with snout
stripes continuous	stripes indistinct or broken	stripes broken above anal fin

WHITE BASS

Morone chrysops

Other Names: silver bass, streaker, lake bass, sand bass

Habitat: large lakes, rivers, and impoundments with relatively clear water

Range: Great Lakes region to the eastern seaboard, through the southeast to the Gulf, west to Texas; Michigan—Lake Michigan, Lake St. Clair, Lake Erie, and Lake Huron

Food: small fish

Reproduction: It spawns in open water over gravel beds or rubble in 6 to 10 feet of water when temperatures reach 55 to 70 degrees; a single female may produce more than 500,000 eggs.

Record and Average Size: Michigan State Record—6.44 lb., 21.9 in.; Average Size—1 to 2 lb., 8 to 10 in.

Fishing Tip: Cast imitation minnow lures into river eddies in the spring.

Notes: White Bass inhabit Michigan's large rivers and lakes but are not found far inland in Michigan. A willing striker, the White Bass is a hard fighter and has good table quality. They have dry flesh, and the flavor and texture can be improved if the fish are quickly put on ice. White Bass travel in large schools, often near the surface, and can be spotted by watching for seagulls feeding on frightened baitfish that are fleeing the marauding predators.

Description: olive to blackish green back; silver-green sides with no stripes; front spiny dorsal fin connected by a small membrane to the soft-rayed back portion

Similar Species: White Bass (pg. 154), Yellow Bass

White Perch

no horizontal stripes except on lateral line

White Bass

black horizontal stripes

Yellow Bass

stripes broken above anal fin

WHITE PERCH

Morone americana

Other Names: narrow-mouth bass; silver or sea perch

Habitat: brackish water in coastal areas; near-shore areas of the Great Lakes; expanding its range into smaller freshwater lakes and rivers

Range: central Mississippi River drainage south to the Gulf of Mexico, Atlantic Coast from Maine to South Carolina; Michigan—Lake Superior, Lake Michigan, Lake Erie, Lake Huron, and Lake St. Clair

Food: fish eggs, minnows, insects, crustaceans

Reproduction: It spawns in late spring over gravel bars of tributary streams.

Record and Average Size: Michigan State Record—2 lb., 13.57 in.; Average Size—6 to 16 oz., 6 to 8 in.

Fishing ⬤ Tip: Fish small white jigs near the bottom for larger perch.

Notes: The White Perch is a coastal Atlantic species that entered the Great Lakes in the 1950s and by the mid-1980s reached the Michigan waters of the Great Lakes. In 1988 it was found in the Chicago area and from there has moved into the Upper Mississippi River system. Fish eggs comprise 100% of the White Perch's diet in the spring, and the species has been linked to Walleye declines in some Canadian waters. White Perch are a popular panfish in some parts of the Great Lakes and are commercially harvested in Lake Erie.

Description: silvery overall, with an almost transparent appearance; mottled brown, tan, or greenish with dark spots on sides; adipose fin; single dorsal fin with two spines and 10 to 11 rays

Similar Species: Yellow Perch (pg. 80), Walleye (pg. 78)

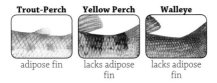

Trout-Perch	Yellow Perch	Walleye
adipose fin	lacks adipose fin	lacks adipose fin

TROUT-PERCH

Percopsis omiscomaycus

Percopsidae

Other Names: grounder, sand minnow

Habitat: prefers clear to slightly turbid (cloudy) water over sand or gravel; avoids soft-bottomed shallows

Range: east-central US through Canada to Alaska; Michigan—Great Lakes and tributary streams

Food: insects, copepods, small fish

Reproduction: It spawns from May to August over sand bars and rocks in lakes and tributary streams.

Record and Average Size: Michigan State Record—none; Average Size—3 to 5 in.

Fishing ⬤ Tip: A good baitfish, but seining is only productive in shallow water at night.

Notes: There are only two species of Trout-Perch and they are restricted to the freshwater of North America. Michigan's lone Trout-Perch species is a deep-water fish that is seldom seen unless it washes up on a beach (where they are sometimes thought to be small walleyes). Nocturnal migration patterns bring large schools into the shallows to feed under the cover of darkness. It is an important forage species for Walleye, Northern Pike, and Lake Trout.

GLOSSARY

adipose fin a small, fleshy fin without rays, located on the midline of the fish's back between the dorsal fin and the tail

air bladder a balloon-like organ located in the gut area of a fish, used to control buoyancy—and in the respiration of some species such as gar; also called "swim bladder" or "gas bladder"

alevin a newly hatched fish that still has its yolk sac

anadromous a fish that hatches in fresh water, migrates to the ocean, then re-enters streams or rivers from the sea (or large inland body of water) to spawn

anal fin a single fin located on the bottom of the fish near the tail

annulus a mark or ring on the scales, spine, vertebrae, or otoliths that scientists use to determine a fish's age

anterior toward the front of a fish, opposite of posterior

bands horizontal marks running lengthwise along the side of a fish

barbel thread-like sensory structures on a fish's head, often near the mouth, commonly called "whiskers"; used for taste or smell

bars vertical markings on the side of a fish

benthic organisms living in or on the bottom

brood swarm a large group or "cloud" of young fish, such as bullheads

cardiform teeth small teeth on the lips of catfish

carnivore a fish that feeds on other fish (also called a piscivore) or animals

catadromous a fish that lives in fresh water and migrates into saltwater to spawn, such as the American Eel

caudal fin the tail or tail fin

caudal peduncle the portion of the fish's body located between the anal fin and the beginning of the tail

coldwater referring to a species or environment; in fish, often a species of trout or salmon found in water that rarely exceeds 70 degrees; also used to describe a lake or river according to average summer temperature

copepod a small (less than 2 mm) crustacean that is part of the zooplankton community

crustacean a crayfish, water flea, crab, or other animal belonging to group of mostly aquatic species that have paired antennae, jointed legs, and an exterior skeleton (exoskeleton); common food for many fish

dorsal relating to the top of the fish, on or near the back; opposite of the ventral, or lower, part of the fish

dorsal fin the fin or fins located along the top of a fish's back

eddy a circular water current, often created by an obstruction

exotic a foreign species, not native to a watershed, such as Zebra Mussel

fingerling a juvenile fish, generally 1 to 10 inches in length, in its first year of life

fork length the overall length of a fish from the mouth to the deepest part of the tail notch

fry a recently hatched young fish that has already absorbed its yolk sac

game fish a species regulated by laws for recreational fishing

gills organs used in aquatic respiration

gill cover large bone covering the gills, also called opercle or operculum

gill raker a comb-like projection from the gill arch

harvest fish that are caught and kept by sport or commercial anglers

ichthyologist a scientist who studies fish

invertebrates animals without backbones, such as insects, crayfish, leeches, and earthworms

lateral line a series of pored scales along the side of a fish that contains organs used to detect vibrations

mollusk an invertebrate with a smooth, soft body such as a clam and snail

native an indigenous or naturally occurring species

omnivore a fish or animal that eats plants and animal matter

otolith an L-shaped bone found in the inner ear of fish

opercle the bone covering the gills, also called the gill cover or operculum

panfish small freshwater game fish that can be fried whole in a pan, such as crappies, perch, and sunfish

pectoral fins paired fins on the side of the fish just behind the gills

pelvic fins paired fins below or behind the pectoral fins on the bottom (ventral portion) of the fish

pharyngeal teeth tooth-like structures found in the throat on the margins of gill bars

plankton floating or weakly swimming aquatic plants and animals, including larval fish, that drift with the current; often eaten by fish; individual organisms are called plankters

range the geographic region in which a species is found

ray, hard supporting part of the fin; resembles a spine but is jointed (can be raised and lowered) and is barbed; found in catfish, carp, and goldfish

ray, soft flexible structures supporting the fin membrane, sometimes branched

scales small, flat plates covering the outer skin of many fish

silt small, easily disturbed bottom particles smaller than sand but larger than clay

siltation the accumulation of soil particles

spawning the process of fish reproduction; involves females laying eggs and males fertilizing them to produce young fish

spines stiff, non-jointed structures found with soft rays in some fins

spiracle an opening on the posterior portion of the head above and behind the eye

standard length length of the fish from the mouth to the end of the vertebral column

stocking the purposeful, artificial introduction of a fish species into an area

swim bladder see air bladder

tapetum lucidum reflective layer of pigment in the eye of Walleyes

terminal mouth a type of mouth that faces forward

total length the length of the fish from the mouth to the tail compressed to its fullest length

tributary a stream that feeds into another stream, river, or lake

turbid cloudy; water clouded by suspended sediments or plant matter that limits visibility and the passage of light

vent the opening at the end of the digestive tract

ventral the underside of the fish; the opposite of dorsal

vertebrate an animal with a backbone

vomerine teeth found on the roof of the mouth

warmwater a non-salmonid species of fish that lives in water that routinely exceeds 70 degrees; also used to describe a lake or river according to average summer temperature

yolk the part of an egg containing food for the developing fish

zooplankton the animal component of plankton; tiny animals that float or swim weakly; common food of fry and small fish

PRIMARY REFERENCES

Bailey, R. M., and W. C. Latta, G. R. Smith. 2004
An Atlas of Michigan Fishes with Keys and Illustrations for Their Identification
University of Michigan Press

Becker, G. C. 1983
Fishes of Wisconsin
University of Wisconsin Press

Eddy, S., and J. C. Underhill. 1974
Northern Fishes
University of Minnesota Press

Hubbs, C. L., and K. F. Lagler. 1958
Fishes of the Great Lakes Region
University of Michigan Press

McClane, A. J. 1978
McClane's Field Guide to Freshwater Fishes of North America
Henry Holt and Company

Phillips, Gary L., and W. D. Schmid, J. C. Underhill. 1982
Fishes of the Minnesota Region
University of Minnesota Press

INDEX

H

I

J

K

L

M

ABOUT THE AUTHOR

Dave Bosanko was born in Kansas and studied engineering before following his love of nature to degrees in biology and chemistry from Emporia State University. He spent thirty years as staff biologist at two of the University of Minnesota's field stations. Though his training was in mammal physiology, Dave worked on a wide range of research projects, from fish, bird, and mammal population studies to experiments with biodiversity and prairie restoration. An avid fisherman and naturalist, he has long enjoyed applying the fruits of his extensive field research to patterning fish location and behavior, and then observing how these fascinating species interact with one another in the underwater web of life.